Joseph Story
and the Comity
of Errors

Joseph Story and the Comity of Errors

A Case Study in Conflict of Laws

Alan Watson

The University of Georgia Press   *Athens and London*

© 1992 by the University of Georgia Press
Athens, Georgia 30602
All rights reserved
Designed by Mary Mendell
Set in Berkeley Medium by Tseng Information
Systems, Inc.
Printed and bound by Thomson-Shore, Inc.
The paper in this book meets the guidelines for
permanence and durability of the Committee
on Production Guidelines for Book Longevity of
the Council on Library Resources.
Printed in the United States of America
96 95 94 93 92 C 5 4 3 2 1

Library of Congress Cataloging in Publication Data
Watson, Alan.
Joseph Story and the comity of errors : a case study in
conflict of laws / Alan Watson.
p.   cm.
Includes index.
ISBN 0-8203-1406-4 (alk. paper)
1. Conflict of laws—History. 2. Story, Joseph, 1779–
1845—Views on comity of nations. 3. Huber, Ulrik,
1636–1694—Views on comity of nations. 4. Comity
of nations. 5. Sociological jurisprudence. I. Title.
K7030.W37   1992
340.9—dc20   91-26989 CIP
British Library Cataloging in Publication Data
available

For David Yalden-Thomson;
for Gary Francione

Contents

Preface

In former times American courts were inclined to take greater notice of the views of legal scholars, such as James Kent, and American jurists and courts took note of continental legal scholarship. It was thus possible for legal rules, even a whole body of law, to be developed by American case law from a foundation in European legal scholarship. The most famous example in the literature is conflict of laws, where, it is accepted, the basic doctrines were built up by the courts on the basis of Joseph Story's general maxims, which he expressly took from the Frisian Ulrich Huber (1635–1694). The central doctrine was "comity of nations," which was to play an important role in landmark decisions such as that of the U.S. Supreme Court in *Dred Scott v. Sandford*, the *Dred Scott* case. One purpose of this book is to show that Story misunderstood the views of Huber on comity; that earlier cases in England and the United States had already accepted Huber; and that subsequent important cases based on Story would have been decided differently if Huber had been followed. Indeed, on Huber's theory the *Dred Scott* case, with all its consequences, could not have arisen.

The book is equally a case study on legal growth and the relationship of law to society. Why was Huber, and not other continental jurists (who were more favored in civil-law systems), treated as authority in common-law jurisdictions? How did it happen that the civilian jurisdiction, Louisiana, played a major role in the deformation of the common law? Why did Story misstate Huber? The answers to such questions will show that conflict of laws in the United States and England developed on the basis of the legal culture of judges and legal scholars. The input of society was slight, but the impact on society was great.

My colleague, Julian McDonnell, teases that I subscribe to the "accident theory" of legal development. No, but "accidents," when a development is based on misunderstanding, are revealing. They highlight the parameters of legal thinking and reasoning, whether of legislators, judges, or jurists. Consequently, they illuminate the absence of fit that there may be between a society and its law.[1]

There were two strands to conflicts law in the United States in the nineteenth century. The first concerns the recognition in each State of the public acts and judicial decisions of every other State.[2] This strand emerged primarily from art. IV, sec. 1, of the U.S. Constitution, the "Full Faith and Credit" clause; it presents few problems and is only incidentally mentioned in this book.[3] The second strand deals with the question of which law is to be applied in a lawsuit, that of the jurisdiction in which the action is brought or that of another jurisdiction which is somehow relevant to the facts of the case. It is this second, and more complex, strand, often called "choice of law," that is the concern of this book.[4]

I have not taken "choice of law" issues in time beyond *Dred Scott*—see, however, appendix C—but the subsequent history is as fascinating, as complex, as full of misunderstandings of previous authorities, as that described here. Foreign jurists, such as Friedrich Carl von Savigny and Ludwig von Bar, continued to have an impact on American scholarship. New approaches, particularly that of Joseph H. Beale, dominated for a time, to be subsequently totally rejected by scholars such as Walter Wheeler Cook and Ernest Lorenzen. Now their view of conflicts law is under attack from neoformalists, notably Lea Brilmayer. Story and Huber's axiom 2 figure in a 1990 U.S. Supreme Court case, *Burnham v. Superior Court, Marin County,* 110 S. Ct. 2105 (1990), for the proposition that the courts of a State have jurisdiction over nonresidents who are physically present in the State. That case promises to usher in an exciting decade.[5] The time seems opportune for a reconsideration of Joseph Story and comity.

Acknowledgments

The manuscript, in various stages of draft, was read at least once by John Cairns, William W. Fisher, John Hart, Peter Hoffer, James Q. Whitman, William M. Wiecek, and Elise Zoli, all of whom gave me sustained, constructive criticism. Much-needed help was given on particular issues by Michael Hoeflich, William Kelly, James C. Oldham, and Phillip Paludan. I also wish to thank the participants in the Harvard Law School Legal History Program, who, on 7 January 1991, having read an early draft, gave vent to lively and helpful criticism.

I needed much library help for this book, and more than could be reasonably expected was provided by everyone at the University of Georgia Law School Library. In particular, Sally Curtis AsKew guided me through the intricacies of citation of early American cases.

Kay Bramlett was, throughout, the perfect secretary.

I dedicate the book to two friends of long standing who, different as they are, are closely linked, and have had a great impact on my life.

I am grateful to all.

Joseph Story
and the Comity
of Errors

1 Ulrich Huber and Comity

Conflict of laws is that part of a state's law which deals with situations in which relevant facts have a connection with another legal system—situations, consequently, which raise problems as to which law is to be applied, that of the territory in which the issue is raised, or that of the other jurisdiction. It is very much at the cutting edge of law, both jurisprudentially and practically, especially perhaps in a federal nation, such as the United States. It became vigorously, intellectually, alive in the United States in Louisiana in 1827 and 1828.[1] In the former year, in the case of *Saul v. His Creditors,* Judge Alexander Porter examined the complexities of continental doctrine in territorial and personal statutes, "a subject, the most intricate and perplexed of any that has occupied the attention of lawyers and courts,"[2] and opined:

> If the subject had been susceptible of clear and positive rules, we may safely believe this illustrious man [D'Argentré][3] would not have left it in doubt, for if any thing be more remarkable in him than his genius and his knowledge, it is the extraordinary fulness and clearness with which he expresses himself on all questions of jurisprudence. When he, therefore, and so many other men, of great talents and learning are thus found to fail in fixing certain principles, we are forced to conclude that they have failed, not from want of ability, but because the matter was not susceptible of being settled on certain principles. They have attempted to go too far. To

define and fix that which cannot, in the nature of things, be defined and fixed. They seem to have forgotten, that they wrote on a question which touched the comity of nations, and that that comity is, and ever must be uncertain. That it must necessarily depend on a variety of circumstances, which cannot be reduced within any certain rule. That no nation will suffer the laws of another to interfere with her own, to the injury of her citizens: that whether they do or not, must depend on the condition of the country in which the foreign law is sought to be enforced—the particular nature of her legislation—her policy—and the character of her institutions. That in the conflict of laws, it must be often a matter of doubt which should prevail, and that whenever that doubt does exist, the court which decides, will prefer the law of its own country, to that of the stranger.[4]

This opinion called forth in the following year a response from Samuel Livermore, who had been a counsellor on the losing side of the case, in his *Dissertations on the Questions Which Arise from the Contrariety of the Positive Laws of Different States and Nations* (New Orleans, 1828).[5] Livermore declared that difficulty in finding general principles in conflict of laws did not point to impossibility, and he rejected the notion of comity.[6] His irritation with Judge Porter is made apparent.

Conflict of laws already had a glorious history in continental Europe. Though scarcely adumbrated upon in Roman law,[7] it had, from the famous Bartolus (1314–1357) onward, attracted the attention of the greatest scholars, especially in Italy, France, and the Netherlands.[8] The multiplicity of city-states in Italy, of local customs in France, the seven states of the United Provinces in the Dutch Republic (and the various local customs), each with its own legal system, early raised the difficult issue of the law to be applied when a case arose which had extraterritorial implications. Naturally, one theory drew upon others, always with its own variations. But in the present context we will need to consider only one, that of the Frisian Ulrich Huber (1635–1694), who was the one jurist above all continually cited in Anglo-American cases and who received the approbation of Joseph Story, the prime architect of nineteenth-century American conflicts law. He does not appear in Judge Porter's judgment, nor in Livermore's historical survey of the scholars of the past. Huber does, however, appear, slightingly, later on in Livermore's account: rather surprising treatment, because Huber might have provided Livermore with his best argument, both in his book and in the case of *Saul v. His Creditors*.[9]

Things were different in the common-law countries. England was remarkably bereft of legal scholars in general until the nineteenth century. Moreover, conflict of laws was not really discussed in common-law courts until the time of Lords Hardwicke and Mansfield in the eighteenth century, primarily as a result of issues of jurisdiction.[10] But when the English, and the Americans, and the Scots had to face the issue of conflict of laws, their great hero was Huber.

To come at length, then, to Ulrich Huber. Huber was very much a Frisian and during his teaching career—he was a judge for three years in Friesland—remained a faithful professor of the University of Franeker, twice rejecting professorships at Leiden. His reputation was enormous and extended well beyond Friesland, attracting many students from other places, especially from Holland, Germany, and Scotland.[11] His main treatment of conflicts law is in a few pages of the second volume of his *Praelectiones juris romani et hodierni* (Lectures on Roman and contemporary law; 1689 is the date of the first edition of the relevant second volume), 2.1.3, which, like the first volume, was presumably written when he was a professor at Franeker.[12] Volume 1 of the *Praelectiones* was devoted to Justinian's *Institutes*, and he turned to the *Digest* in volume 2. So his treatment of conflict of laws is right at the beginning of his commentary on the *Digest*.

Huber claims in his section 1 that there is nothing on conflict of laws in Roman law, but that nonetheless the fundamental rules by which this system should be determined must be sought in Roman law, though the issue relates more to the *ius gentium* than the *ius civile*. These two terms had more than one meaning in the Roman legal sources, but Huber is using them in this context in the sense found in Justinian's *Institutes* 1.2.1. *Ius civile* is law which each people has established for itself and is particular to itself. *Ius gentium* is declared at this point in the *Institutes* to be law established by reason among all men and observed equally by all nations. In fact, for an institution to be characterized in this sense as belonging to the *ius gentium* it seems to be enough that it is accepted at Rome and other states. *Ius gentium* in this context is very much part of Roman private law. It should be stressed that Huber here is not using *ius gentium* in the sense of "law established between peoples," that is, international law. Though that was one meaning in Huber's own time, the term *ius gentium* was not so used in Roman law. Huber goes on: "In order to lay bare the subtlety of this particularly intricate question we will set out three axioms which being accepted, as undoubtedly it appears they must be, seem to make straightforward the way to the remaining issues."[13] At the beginning of the first volume of his *Praelectiones*, Huber had explained what he meant by axioms. Budaeus,[14] he declared, had not absurdly said that rules of law were handed down by *axiomata* or by *positiones,* terms that he said were taken from the usage of mathematicians.[15] "For axioms are nothing other than statements that require no proof." Their correctness is thus self-evident.

Accordingly, conflict of laws as a system exists for Huber only if one accepts, as he feels and says we must, his three axioms (which significantly he prints in italics in section 2). As axioms they require no proof. The first two he expressly and reasonably—according to the approach of his time—bases on Roman law, on *Digest* 2.1.20 and *Digest* 48.22.7.10, respectively. The first axiom is, "*The laws of each sovereign authority have force within the boundaries of its state, and bind all subject to it, but not beyond.*"[16] The second reads: "*Those people are held to be subject to a sovereign authority who are found within its boundaries, whether they are there permanently or temporarily.*"[17] The third axiom is referred to no such authority but is Huber's own contribution. It must for Huber be treated, like the other two, as a binding rule, in order to have a systematic basis for conflict of laws. It reads: *The rulers of states so act from comity* (comiter) *that the rights of each people exercised within its own boundaries should retain their force everywhere, insofar as they do not prejudice the power or rights of another state or its citizens.*[18]

The absence of stated authority for the third axiom does not mean that for Huber there was no authority for it. Indeed, he has already stated that the fundamental rules for the subject have to be sought in Roman law. The position for Huber is that by Roman law axiom 3 is part of the *ius gentium*—because it is accepted among all peoples—and so it need not be expressly set out in any particular jurisdiction—Rome, for instance—in order to be valid there.[19] In fact, as we shall see, Huber goes on to claim in the same section of his work that no doubt has ever existed as to the validity of the third axiom. (This is not true except in a perverted sense, since Huber seems to be the architect of the scope of the axiom). Though axiom 3 is not stated by Huber in a normative way, it is for him a rule of law, and is normative. That is the very nature of an axiom.

This course of reasoning is entirely appropriate for Huber. He is attempting to set out the principles on which a particular branch of law, namely conflict of laws, is established. For this he does require authority. Roman law was looked to in all continental European countries to supply legal authority in general. Its status varied from jurisdiction to jurisdiction, though notoriously there had been a greater reception of Roman law in Friesland than elsewhere in the United Provinces.[20] But Huber is not here concerned particularly with the law of Friesland. He is actually attempting to set out the principles which all states are bound to apply in conflicts situations. The only principles that could be binding, not in one territory alone but everywhere, had to be drawn from Roman law. There just was no other appropriate system. For the Romans, *ius gentium*, law that was accepted everywhere, was ipso facto part of Roman law. Therefore, if the validity of axiom 3 has not been doubted (as Huber claims), it is part of Roman private law; and it is as Roman law that it is authoritative. Huber is not out of line with other scholars in this approach. In exactly the same way, when Bartolus was earlier attempting to build up a system of conflicts law, he based (or purported to base) his propositions on Roman law.

One example may stand for all to illustrate this style of reasoning in Bartolus.[21] He says:

> Many questions may be solved by what has been said above. There is a statute at Assisi, where the contract of dowry and marriage was celebrated, that if the wife died without children the husband should enjoy a third part of the dowry. But in this city of Perugia, from which the husband comes, there is a statute that the husband should enjoy one half. Which law will be regarded? Certainly it is the law of the domicile of the husband: in accordance with *Digest* 5.1.65.[22]

The *Digest* passage cited runs:

> A wife should sue for her dowry in the place where the husband had his home, not where the dotal instrument was drawn up. For this is not the type of contract in which that place where the instrument of dowry was made ought to be regarded, rather than that man to

whose home the woman herself would return under the conditions of the marriage.[23]

Prima facie, the *Digest* text of Ulpian is authority for the proposition of Bartolus. But Ulpian is actually making a very different point. Let us consider Bartolus's example under Roman law in the time of Ulpian. Then, the law in force in any two towns, such as Assisi and Perugia, within the Roman empire would be one and the same: Roman law. The issue for Ulpian, and for Justinian in the *Digest*, was not which city's law was applicable, because it would always be the same law. The issue was in which city the wife ought to bring her lawsuit. Exactly that issue would arise in many contexts. A merchant from Narni agreed in Spoleto with a pottery maker from Rieti to purchase wine jars to be delivered at Ostia for shipment to Alexandria, and the pottery maker failed to deliver. Should the merchant bring suit in Narni, Spoleto, Rieti, Ostia, or Alexandria? The law to be applied would in all instances be the same: there is no issue of conflicts of law. But the convenience of the parties would be greatly affected by the choice of venue, and rules did develop to decide the issue of which town had jurisdiction.

If Bartolus had been writing a treatise on Roman law, then his approach (and that of Huber) to the texts would be wrong. But that is not what Bartolus was doing. He was using Roman legal texts as the only authority he had (in the absence of local custom or statute) to build up a new area of law. By the canons of legal reasoning that were regarded as appropriate, he properly cited a *Digest* text out of context to get the result he favored.

It goes without saying, of course, that Huber's axiom 3 was not found in Roman law. Nor, of course, were axioms 1 and 2 a part of a system of conflicts law, but concerned issues of jurisdiction. Huber was well aware of this and did not hide the fact, since he had said in this very same paragraph that Roman law had nothing on this subject. But this mode of reasoning from Roman law to build up new law unknown to the Romans was standard juristic practice.[24] Indeed, in the absence of other authority, it was necessary if law was to grow. It is important to determine the precise meaning of axiom 3 for Huber. It is fully in accordance with the interpretation so far given of Huber's words that he proceeds: "From this it is clear that this subject is to be sought not from the uncompounded civil law (*ius civile*) but from the benefits and tacit agreement of peoples: because just as the laws of one people cannot have direct force among another, so nothing could be more inconvenient than that what is valid by the law of a certain place be rendered invalid by a difference in law in another place. This is the reason for the third axiom on which hitherto there has been no doubt."[25]

That Huber regarded the application of foreign law as binding becomes even clearer when we bring into account his earliest treatment of the subject in the second edition of his *De jure civitatis* (On the law of the state), published in 1684 at 3.10.1: "Among the matters that different peoples reciprocally owe one another is properly included the observance of laws of other states in other realms. To which, even if they are not bound by agreement or the necessity of being subordinate, nonetheless, the rationale of common intercourse between peoples demands mutual indulgence in this area."[26] By *ius gentium* in its other, non-Roman, sense of "international law"—and that sense is also relevant for this passage—one state is bound to observe the law of another, first if it is subject to it, second if there is an agreement to that effect. That was well established. In addition, for Huber, one state is equally bound to observe the law of another on a further rationale which is, namely, comity.

It is the application of axiom 3 as a binding rule of law that gives private law transnational force. The laws of a state do not directly apply outside the territory of the state, but the rulers of other states must apply them *comiter* even when their own rules are different.

There is admirably skillful sleight-of-hand in all this. Huber's axiom 3 did not exist in Roman law, and this he admits even though he bases his whole system supposedly on Roman law. But then he claims his axiom 3 has never been doubted and is part of the *ius gentium,* accepted everywhere. In an upside-down sense, the first part of his claim is perfectly accurate. Axiom 3 had never been expressed before and hence was never doubted! As we shall see, other Dutch jurists had a very different notion of *comitas.* Huber provides no evidence that *comitas* in his sense was part of the *ius gentium,* accepted everywhere. And, of course, he cannot provide such evidence because his view is novel. But he is not required to provide any evidence because he sets out his legal proposition in an axiom, and by his definition an axiom is a rule that requires no proof because it is self-evident.

Huber's aim was to provide conflict of laws with a legal basis. Axiom 3 determines when and whether a state can raise an exception to recognizing that the law of another jurisdiction rules: it is not to be up to the individual court to be able to reject the foreign law because it finds it unpalatable or prefers its own rules.

I have emphasized that for Huber axiom 3 is a rule of law because his use of the word *comiter* may easily mislead and, as we shall see, has often misled. In classical Latin the word *comitas,* from which *comiter* derives, meant something akin to "courtesy." Its precise meaning in later Latin, and among medieval and later jurists, is not easy to establish, but in fact need not detain us. The best account of it is that of the Dutch scholar, E. M. Meijers, who points out very correctly that expressions like *de comitate* are always opposed to expressions like *de iure* (by law). *Comitas* as a word used in this connection first appears in Paulus Voet, *De statutis eorumque concursu* (On statutes and their ranking), which was published in 1661 at Amsterdam, and for him the term "indicates that a state, following a neighbor's law, does not act because the rule is binding on it by strict necessity of law."[27] By itself, the word *comitas* does not indicate a binding obligation.

Huber's use of the term *comiter* is actually similar. His axioms 1 and 2 are to the effect that the laws of a state are not directly binding beyond its territory. Axiom 3 states that, subject to the exception stated in it, rulers are bound to apply foreign law *comiter,* by comity. Foreign law is thus binding, but indirectly, so there is no conflict between axioms 1 and 2 on the one hand and axiom 3 on the other. But in order to understand Huber, it is a mistake to treat *comiter* out of context as has often been done. It is not that rulers act *comiter* and enforce foreign law as far as seems reasonable and right, but that rulers must act *comiter* in order to enforce foreign law that is not directly binding in their territory. Meijers writes: "Thus, the idea of the Dutch authors, with their *comitas gentium* is nothing other than this: each state is its own master to decide the extent to which it will apply a foreign law."[28] This is emphatically not the position of Huber. He does not allow for free discretion in applying foreign law. At the beginning of his next section, 3, he writes, again with italics:

> This proposition flows from the above: *All transactions and acts both in court and extrajudicial, whether in contemplation of death or inter vivos, properly executed according to the law of a particular place are*

valid even where a different law prevails, and where if they were performed as they were performed they would have been invalid. And, on the other hand, transactions and acts executed in a particular place contrary to the laws of that place, since they are invalid from the beginning, cannot be valid anywhere.[29]

Foreign law is binding. Of course, since it is binding only indirectly, whereas the law of the local jurisdiction is binding directly, foreign law would not prevail where it was expressly excluded by the local law, say by statute. This is not stated by Huber, but it is implicit in the distinction he makes between axioms 1 and 2 on the one hand, and axiom 3 on the other.

This necessary recognition of foreign law is, of course, subject to the exception to axiom 3: transactions and acts elsewhere are recognized "insofar as they do not prejudice the power or rights of another state or its citizens." In keeping with the brevity of axioms, the practical meaning of the exception requires elucidation. Huber glosses it a little further on in section 3: "But it is subject to this exception: if the rulers of another people would thereby suffer a serious inconvenience they would not be bound to give effect to such acts and transactions, according to the limitation of the third axiom. The point deserves to be explained by examples."[30] The examples he gives here and in another work, *Heedensdaegse Rechtsgeleertheyt* (Contemporary jurisprudence, 1686), best clarify Huber's meaning. The situations mentioned as giving rise to the exception can be fitted into a very small number of distinct classes, but before we examine these we should look at a situation that appears anomalous, yet is not in fact part of the exception.

The basic rule for Huber is that the validity and rules of a contract depend upon the place where the contract was made. Likewise, if a marriage is lawful in the state where it was contracted and celebrated, it will be valid everywhere (subject to any exception in axiom 3). But this is dependent, as Huber notes in section 10, on a fiction of Roman law that is set out in *Digest* 44.7.21:[31] "Everyone is considered to have contracted in that place in which he is bound to perform."[32] Hence, for marriage, for instance, the place of a marriage contract is not where the marriage contract was entered into, but where the parties intend to conduct the marriage, which will be the normal residence of the parties. This can, of course, have an important effect on community of property and other property relations of the spouses, but the effect does not follow from the exception to axiom 3.

A first category within the exception is where persons subject to a jurisdiction take themselves out of the territory deliberately in order to avoid the jurisdiction. Most examples would amount to a *fraus legis*. The following instances occur in Huber. Where a Frisian, who is forbidden by law to marry his niece, goes with a niece deliberately to Brabant and marries her, the marriage will not be recognized in Friesland. (On the other hand, when someone from Brabant marries there within the prohibited degrees under a papal dispensation, and the spouses migrate to Friesland, the marriage that was valid in Brabant remains valid).[33] Where young persons under guardianship in West Friesland go to East Friesland to marry, where consent of guardians is not required, and then immediately return to West Friesland, the marriage is void as a subversion of the law. Again, if goods are sold in one place for delivery in another where they are prohibited, the buyer is not bound in the latter place because of the exception.[34] An instance that occasioned Huber difficulty is recorded in section 6:

> Titius struck a man on the head within the boundaries of Friesland. He died the following night having lost much blood through his nostrils, but having drunk and eaten well. Titius, I say, escaped into Overyssel. There he was apprehended, apparently at his volition; he was quickly tried and acquitted on the ground that the man had not died from the wound. This judgment is sent to Friesland and absolution is sought for the acquitted defendant. Although the reason for acquittal was not foreign to the truth, the court of Friesland nonetheless had difficulty in granting validity to the decision and pardon to the accused, although this was demanded by the people of Overyssel. Because with such an escape into neighboring territory and feigned proceedings, the way seemed too open for evading the Frisian jurisdiction which is the basis for the exception to the third axiom.[35]

The substantive issue was one of causation. Germanic states differed on the subject. Some states took a harder line than others on when there was a break in the chain of causation; did a wound cause death when the victim was dilatory in seeking medical aid; or when the doctor was remiss in treatment; or when the victim was insufficiently prudent, as by eating or drinking too much; or when time elapsed between the wounding and the death?[36] Here the substantive law differed between Overyssel and Friesland. The Frisian Huber has sympathy with the Overyssel substantive law. But he seems in favor of not recognizing the Overyssel verdict because of *fraus legis:* it prejudices the power of Friesland. What is significant for us in this choice of example is that, as Huber makes clear, his objection to giving recognition to the foreign law is not based on any feeling that the substance of the law is immoral. An important part of the problem was that in Huber's time extradition was allowed only on the basis of *humanitas,* that is, not on the basis of any legal right. In such a case a written guarantee was to be given to the extraditing magistrate that the act would not be prejudicial to the jurisdiction of the extraditing state. Paulus Voet reports that this was received doctrine in the United Provinces.[37]

A second category for the exception is also of limited extent. If two or more contracts are made in different states and the rights of creditors would vary in different states according to the priority or value accorded to each contract, the sovereign need not, and indeed cannot, extend the law of the foreign territory to the prejudice of his own citizens.[38] For instance, some states give validity to the pledge of property without delivery; others require delivery for a valid hypothec. If state A does not demand delivery, and a pledge is made there without delivery, and the issue comes somehow before the court of state B, state B in the ordinary case would recognize the hypothec as valid because it was valid in state A. But if the same hypothec is made in state A, a second hypothec with delivery is made in state B to a citizen of B, and the issue comes before the court of B, the court must decide the issue of priority according to its own law, because in the event of a straight conflict of rights, a court cannot extend the law of a foreign state to the detriment of its citizens. In such a case of conflict it is more reasonable, says Huber, to follow one's own law than a foreign law.

The limited scope of this category should be noticed. It exists only when there are at least two contracts, contracted in different territories with different laws, where these contracts have to be pitted against one another, and where one party is a citizen of the state where the case is heard. It should be stressed that even in this case Huber is not deciding against the validity of the contract made abroad. It is valid, but its ranking is postponed behind the contract made in the home territory. Huber gives another example. A marriage contract in Holland contains the private bargain, valid in Holland, that the wife will not be liable for debts subsequently contracted by the husband alone. Such an agreement if made in Friesland would be effective against subsequent creditors of the husband only if it was made public or if the creditors could be expected to have knowledge of it. If the husband subsequently contracted a debt in Friesland, the wife was sued for one-half of the debt, and she pled her marriage contract as a defense. The defense was disallowed in Friesland. By the same token, if the wife had been sued in Holland, the defense would have prevailed. This category for the exception exists only where there are contracts with different bases—though this time the contracts are at one remove from the basic act, the private bargain in the marriage contract—and superior ranking has to be granted to one.

A final category—which, as we shall see, is in theory not within the exception—has special significance within the context of this work. Not its sole significance for us is that Huber graces it with only a single example, in section 8. "Marriage also belongs to these rules. If it is lawful in the place where it was contracted and celebrated, it is valid and effective everywhere, subject to this exception, that it does not prejudice others; to which one should add, unless it is too revolting an example. For instance, if a marriage in the second degree, incestuous according to the law of nations, happened to be allowed anywhere. This could scarcely ever be the case."[39] We have already considered what was meant by "prejudice to others." Now we must consider the nonrecognition of foreign law on the ground that it is "too revolting." To judge from Huber's words in the example, this is permitted only when the foreign law is contrary to the law of nations.[40] Moreover, according to Huber, this will scarcely ever be the case. Accordingly, only very rarely will a state be legally entitled to fail to give recognition to another's law on the basis that it is too revolting or immoral, and then the rejection will be on the basis that the rule is contrary to the law of nations. Since axiom 3 is part of the law of nations, and binding on that account, an act or transaction valid where it is made, but void by the *ius gentium,* will by the same *ius gentium* be given no recognition in another jurisdiction when it would have been void if made there. But it must be emphasized that the invalidity does not derive from the exception to axiom 3 but from the very legal basis of that axiom.

We must stress the very limited extent of the true exceptions to

Huber's axiom 3. The axiom is a rule of law subject to exceptions. But in the axiom itself, the exceptions are stated so widely that they could swallow up the rule. This cannot be Huber's intention because he is adamant that an axiom contains a binding rule. He is also adamant that the scope of his exceptions is to be explained by the examples. Perhaps we should detect in Huber's broadness of language a sensitivity that, as we shall see, his view of the indirect binding nature of the rule of recognition of foreign law was stricter than that of his contemporaries. What should be stressed above all from Huber's examples is that, in comity, courts have no discretion in deciding whether to recognize foreign law or not. That issue is determined by the facts of the case.

That the above-mentioned categories are the only ones for the exception best appears in the context of the fuller treatment in Huber's *Heedendaegse Rechtsgeleertheyt* 1.3:

18. What has been said in these examples with regard to wills, applies also without doubt to transactions between living persons, such as all sorts of contracts, which, if entered into according to the laws and customs of particular places, must hold good everywhere, both *coram lege* and *ex lege,* and even in places where otherwise they are forbidden.

19. For example: It may be forbidden in certain places, as it formerly was here, to sell brandy or certain other commodities; if, however, a citizen of such a country is sued for the price of brandy bought at a place where it might be bought without restriction, he must be adjudged to pay, and that even in those places where it is forbidden to buy and sell such commodities, because the contract, being good where it was made, is everywhere recognized to hold good between the parties.

20. But if the parties had entered into a bargain for the delivery of brandy in the country where it has been forbidden, no action would arise on such a bargain in that country, because it would conflict with the law and authority of that very territory which has forbidden such delivery within its limits.

21. Take another case. A foreigner sold to a Frisian here, and delivered in the Province, brandy or other forbidden commodities. According to law he cannot bring an action anywhere on such a sale, not even outside the Province, should he find the purchaser

there; certainly no action would arise on the sale, because they both did what they were forbidden to do; unless equity on account of special circumstances might provide some extraordinary remedy against the avaricious purchaser.

22. Yet another. It has been forbidden in a certain town to drink brandy. People go just outside the jurisdiction of the town, and drink it there. Although the traffic is legitimate there, yet it gives no ground of claim in that town, because it tends to its signal inconvenience and disorder; elsewhere, however, a claim arises.

23. Once again. It is forbidden to go and drink just outside the jurisdiction of a town, in order not to lessen its duties, an enactment of which instances are known; the citizens do it, however; they are punishable in their own town for this act; but the trade is legitimate, and therefore gives a claim everywhere except in that town, for the reason given in the previous section.[41]

I quote these passages not because the work from which they are taken was influential in the United States—it was not, being written in Dutch —but because they help us to understand Huber. Section 19 tells us that a contract, valid where it was made, is to be recognized elsewhere, even in states that would not permit it within their territory. Section 20 is merely an application of the Roman fiction that Huber adopts that a contract is made where it is to be performed. Section 21 is to the effect that a contract void where it is made is void everywhere. Sections 22 and 23 merely repeat that evasive action to avoid a particular jurisdiction will not be acceptable within that jurisdiction. So Huber's treatment here does not amount to creating a further category within the exception.

We can now restate Huber's axiom 3, with the exceptions. An act or transaction in one state has no direct legal effect beyond the territory of the state, but a state is bound by the law of nations to act *comiter,* courteously, in order to give effect to foreign law in judging the effects of acts or transactions occurring in another state; subject to the sole exceptions that (1) local law will be applied if there has been a deliberate attempt to evade local jurisdiction by one subject to it, (2) local law will be applied where there is more than one act or transaction, one of which occurred locally, and where superiority of transaction depends on which law is applied. In addition, an act valid where it was made (or a status valid by the domicile), but void by the law of nations, is void elsewhere. Again I stress that for Huber the courts had no discretion whether to recognize the foreign law or not. A clinching argument for this proposition, if one were needed, is that nowhere in his discussion does Huber indicate a situation where a court might have a choice.

Behind Huber there stood centuries of European scholarship seeking to create a coherent system of conflict of laws. Variations in theories were great. In Joseph Story's time the difficulty of the subject, even perhaps the impossibility of creating a system, was, as we have seen, a commonplace. Into this preceding scholarship we do not need to go, but I wish to discuss one scholar—and one aspect of his work—who has already been mentioned, Paulus Voet. He is brought in to show the contribution of Huber. Paulus Voet, as already stated, was the earliest jurist to use the terms *comiter* and *comitas* in this connection, and his meaning was very different from that of Huber. Thus, in the section headings of his *De statutis eorumque concursu* he denominates 4.2.17 as "A territorial statute is often observed outside of its territory for comity and equity."[42] Thus, for him there is no obligation to observe such law: it happens often, but it need not happen. The section itself, making the point even clearer, reads: "And so, sometimes, when a neighboring people wishes to observe the customs of a neighbor out of comity, and lest many matters properly accomplished be thrown into confusion, on account of custom statutes migrate beyond the territory of the law maker, when their effect has been examined."[43] Thus, for Voet, it does not always happen that the relevant foreign law is recognized: when it does, it happens only after an examination of the effect of the foreign statute. There is no legal obligation to put the neighboring law into effect. For Voet, in contrast to Huber, courts have discretion. Other passages from the same work confirm this interpretation of Paulus Voet's use of *comiter*.[44] Thus, concerning the force of a foreign decree forbidding someone as a prodigal from dealing with his property, Voet writes: "I would prefer that this should obtain, not so much by force of law as from humanity, that a people observe the decrees of a neighboring people out of comity, to avoid confusion of many matters."[45] In contrast to the view of Huber there is here no legal basis (in the *ius gentium*) for *comitas*. Each nation or state will decide for itself when it will, and when it will not, accept foreign law.

Thus, Voet's conception of *comitas* is that of voluntarily accepting to recognize and apply foreign law. Such a view is shared by other Dutch writers such as his son, Johannes Voet, and Johannes à Sande, and appears even earlier in Simon à Groenewegen, though the terms *comitas* and *comiter* are not used.[46] Its roots are ancient.[47] Story's view of *comitas* is indeed that of Paulus Voet and these other Dutch scholars, though he does not use them in this connection.

Discussing the influence of Huber on English private international law, D. J. Llewelyn Davies wrote: "The doctrine of comity, at most, only provides a theoretical foundation upon which a system of Conflict of Laws may be built. It does not by itself indicate the principles according to which the system is to be constructed."[48] This is true for the doctrine of comity in Story, Paulus Voet, and others. It is quite incorrect for Huber, on whom Story claimed to rely.[49]

Little more is needed to complete Huber's account of conflict of laws. I give the remainder here, not for the sake of completeness, but to indicate the strength of the theory; and I set it at the end of the chapter because in general it is not needed for the main argument of the book.

Although contracts, as we have seen, are governed by the law of the place where they are made, the manner of enforcing the contractual right, issues of prescription and execution, are governed by the law of the place where a remedy is sought.[50] This distinction, attributed to Huber, was accepted in both England and the United States.[51] In one New York case, *Decouche v. Savetier,* counsel in argument even claimed Huber invented the distinction.[52] This is inexact, since it goes back at least as far as Bartolus, who claims to derive it from Justinian's *Digest.*[53]

Although his basic principle is the subjection of persons to the law of the country in which they act, this does not apply with respect to immoveables when they are regarded, not as depending on the free disposition of the individual, but as impressed with characteristics by the state in which they are situated.[54] These immoveables are then governed by the law of the place where they are situated, to avoid general confusion. Therefore a Frisian who owns land in the province of Groningen cannot dispose of it by will, since that is prohibited by the law of Groningen.[55] Huber rightly insists there is no inconsistency here. The will (or contract) is still valid if it is valid where it is made; only it cannot affect immoveables in another jurisdiction contrary to the law of that jurisdiction.[56]

From his three axioms Huber also derived the proposition that personal qualities impressed on someone by the law of a certain place follow him everywhere, to this effect that, in any place whatever, he enjoys and is subject to the law that persons of that class in such other place enjoy or are subject to.[57] Thus, an unemancipated son, resident in Friesland, cannot make a valid will in Friesland. An unemancipated son, resident in Holland, can make a valid will in Holland. An unemancipated son from Friesland acquires in Holland the rights of the general class of un-emancipated sons there, so if he makes a will there the will is valid in Holland. So it would be valid elsewhere, as being valid according to the law of the place where it was made; except that it would not be valid in Friesland because otherwise it would be too easy to go elsewhere to evade the local law.

2 Joseph Story and Comity

I n 1834, when he was Dane Professor of Law at Harvard, Joseph Story published at Boston his *Commentaries on the Conflict of Laws*.[1] In the second chapter, entitled "General Maxims of International Jurisprudence," he adverts "to a few general maxims or axioms, which constitute the basis, upon which all reasonings on the subject must necessarily rest."[2] After some discussion of these he comes to Huber.

> Huberus has laid down three axioms, which he deems sufficient to solve all the intricacies of the subject. The first is, that the laws of every empire have force only within the limits of its own government, and bind all, who are subjected to it, but not beyond those limits. The second is, that all persons, who are found within the limits of a government, whether their residence is permanent or temporary, are to be deemed subjects thereof. The third is, that the rulers of every empire from comity admit, that the laws of every people in force within its own limits, ought to have the same force every where, so far as they do not prejudice the power or rights of other governments, or of their citizens. "From this," he adds, "it appears, that this matter is to be determined, not simply by the civil laws, but by the convenience and tacit consent of different people; for since the laws of one people cannot have any direct force among another people, so nothing could be more inconvenient in the commerce and general intercourse of nations, than that what is valid by

the laws of one place should become without effect by the diversity of laws of another; and that this is the true reason of the last axiom, of which no one hitherto seems to have entertained any doubt."[3]

Story accepted the authority of Huber, against critics such as Hertius and, more particularly, against Livermore.[4] He claimed for Huber that he "has at least this satisfactory foundation for his most important rule, that he is mainly guided in it by the practice of nations; and he thus aimed, as Grotius had done before him, to avail himself of the practice of nations, as a solid proof of the acknowledged law of nations."[5] He continued:

> Some attempts have been made, but without success, to undervalue the authority of Huberus. It is certainly true, that he is not often spoken of, except by jurists belonging to the Dutch School. Boullenois, however, has quoted his third and last axiom with manifest approbation. But it will require very little aid of authority to countenance his merits, if his maxims are well founded; and if they are not, no approbation, founded on foreign recognitions, can disguise their defects. It is not, however, a slight recommendation of his works, that hitherto he has possessed an undisputed preference on this subject over other continental jurists, as well in England as in America. Indeed, his two first maxims will in the present day scarcely be disputed by any one; and the last seems irresistibly to flow from the right and duty of every nation to protect its own subjects against injuries resulting from the unjust and prejudicial influence of foreign laws; and to refuse its aid to carry into effect any foreign laws, which are repugnant to its own interests and polity.[6]

Story's commendation is self-evident. And that Story followed Huber for the basic principles of conflict of laws is believed by all subsequent scholars.[7]

But there can also be no doubt that Story misunderstood or misrepresented Huber. The best evidence comes from the end of the passage just quoted and his own very next paragraphs:

> It is difficult to conceive, upon what ground a claim can be rested, to give to any municipal laws an extra-territorial effect, when those laws are prejudicial to the rights of other nations, or their subjects. It would at once annihilate the sovereignty and equality of the nations, which should be called upon to recognize and en-

force them; or compel them to desert their own proper interest and duty in favour of strangers, who were regardless of both. A claim, so naked of principle and authority to support it, is wholly inadmissible.

It has been thought by some jurists, that the term, "comity," is not sufficiently expressive of the obligation of nations to give effect to foreign laws, when they are not prejudicial to their own rights and interests. And it has been suggested, that the doctrine rests on a deeper foundation; that it is not so much a matter of comity, or courtesy, as of paramount moral duty. Now, assuming, that such a moral duty does exist, it is clearly one of imperfect obligation, like that of beneficence, humanity, and charity. Every nation must be the final judge for itself, not only of the nature and extent of the duty, but of the occasions, on which its exercise may be justly demanded. And, certainly, there can be no pretence to say, that any foreign nation has a right to require the full recognition and execution of its own laws in other territories, when those laws are deemed oppressive or injurious to the rights or interests of the inhabitants of the latter, or where their moral character is questionable, or their provisions impolitic. Even in other cases, it is difficult to perceive a clear foundation in morals, or in natural law, for declaring, that any nation has a right (all others being equal in sovereignty) to insist, that its own positive laws shall be of superior obligation in a foreign realm to the domestic laws of the latter, of an equally positive character. What intrinsic right has one nation to declare, that no contract shall be binding, which is made by any of its subjects in a foreign country, unless they are twenty-five years of age, more than another nation, where the contract is made, to declare, that such contract shall be binding, if made by any persons of twenty-one years of age? One should suppose, that if there be any thing clearly within the scope of national sovereignty, it is the right to fix, what shall be the rule to govern contracts made within its own territories.

That a nation ought not to make its own jurisprudence an instrument of injustice for other nations, or their subjects, may be admitted. But in a vast variety of cases, which may be put, the rejection of the laws of a foreign nation may work less injustice, than the enforcement of them will remedy. And, here again, every nation must judge for itself, what is its true duty in the administration of justice. It is not to be taken for granted, that the rule of the foreign nation is right, and that its own is wrong.

The true foundation, on which the administration of international law must rest, is, that the rules, which are to govern, are those, which arise from mutual interest and utility, from a sense of the inconveniences, which would result from a contrary doctrine, and from a sort of moral necessity to do justice, in order that justice may be done to us in return.[8]

The passage is so clear in itself as almost to require no comment. But perhaps the beginning of the second paragraph should be specially noted. It has been claimed, Story says, that "comity" is not sufficiently suggestive of the obligation to give effect to foreign law and that there is a paramount moral duty to do so. Here he is, of course, referring to Livermore. But if there is such a moral duty, then, urges Story, it is one of imperfect obligation, "like that of beneficence, humanity, and charity." Now the distinction between perfect obligation and imperfect obligation was well known, not only to philosophers, but also to continental jurists, such as Robert Pothier.[9] A perfect obligation is owed to a specific person or body, whether it can be enforced in court or not. The obligation remains perfect, even if it can be enforced only in the forum of conscience. An imperfect obligation is definitely an obligation, but one not due to any person or body specifically, except to God. There is an obligation to be charitable, but not to donate to any particular charity. The obligation is imperfect, and is not owed to any specific person or body. If, however, when in deep distress one was succored by A, and subsequently A became indigent, one would have a perfect obligation toward A, even when this was not actionable in court. But for Story, if it were accepted that there was an obligation above the notion of comity to enforce foreign law, then it would be only an imperfect obligation, not owed to any person or body. Nothing could better illustrate Story's distance from Huber: comity (lesser than this supposed imperfect moral obligation) does not for Story impose a duty to give effect to the law of any particular foreign nation or state. For Huber comity itself gives rise to a perfect obligation; and this is a binding obligation that should be enforced in court, not just in the forum of conscience.

Story says further:

But of the nature, and extent, and utility of this recognition of foreign laws, respecting the state and condition of persons, every nation must judge for itself, and certainly is not bound to recognize them, when they would be prejudicial to its own interests. The very terms, in which the doctrine is commonly enunciated, carry along with them this necessary qualification and limitation of it. Mutual utility presupposes, that the interest of all nations is consulted, and not that of one only. Now, this demonstrates, that the doctrine owes its origin and authority to the voluntary adoption and consent of nations. It is, therefore, in the strictest sense a matter of the comity of nations, and not of absolute paramount obligation, superseding all discretion on the subject.[10]

Thus, Story has taken away from Huber the idea—the one idea that was particularly his—that a state is under an obligation to follow the law of another state where the act or transaction in question occurred, and he has replaced it with the notion that each state should be the judge for itself in deciding when and to what extent foreign law should be recognized, but should so recognize such foreign law from a sense of mutual interest and utility and should do justice in order that justice be done in return. The first passage quoted from Story shows that, when he says "this matter is to be determined, not simply by the civil laws, but by the convenience and tacit consent of different people," he had mis-understood Huber on the nature of the obligation of comity. For Story, the obligation is not imposed by law ("by the civil laws," as he puts it); for Huber, the obligation is a legal obligation deriving from Roman law, not indeed the Roman *ius civile,* particular to the Romans, but the *ius gentium,* binding on all people.

This—Story's—notion of comity is lacking in precision. Indeed, a modern scholar of the subject, Paul Finkelman, writes of "the unen-forceable and unpredictable legal theories of the international law of comity."[11]

We can put the issue another way. On Huber's theory, all nations and States would have the same response to conflict of laws. There would be one system of private international law in the Western world. The effect in each instance would, of course, vary according to the other rules of private law. On Story's theory, there would be no uniformity: conflict of laws would vary from jurisdiction to jurisdiction just like any other branch of private law.

But since comity was the central doctrine for choice of law, one misstatement or misunderstanding of it by Story leads on to another. In the context of contracts he writes:

> But there is an exception to the rule as to the universal validity of contracts, which is, that no nation is bound to recognise or enforce any contracts, which are injurious to their own interests, or to those of their own subjects. This exception results from the consideration, that the authority of the acts and contracts done in other states, as well as the laws, by which they are regulated, are not, *proprio vigore,* of any efficacy beyond the territories of that state; and whatever is attributed to them elsewhere, is from comity, and not of strict right. And every independent community will, and ought to judge for itself, how far that comity ought to extend. The reasonable limitation is, that it shall not suffer prejudice by its comity.[12] Mr. Justice Best has with great force said, that in cases turning upon the comity of nations (*comitas inter communitates*), it is a maxim, that the comity cannot prevail in cases, where it violates the law of our own country, the law of nature, or the law of God. Contracts, therefore, which are in evasion or fraud of the laws of a country, or the rights or duties of its subjects, contracts against good morals, or religion, or public rights, and contracts opposed to the national policy or institutions, are deemed nullities in every country, affected by such considerations; although they may be valid by the laws of the place, where they are made.[13]

Here he is restating the position that we have already seen him take.

The English case involving Mr. Justice Best dates from 1824, *Forbes v. Cochrane,* 2 B. & C. 448, and Story, who cites it after the word "God," refers specifically to page 471. The issue in the case which concerns us was whether, when slaves in a foreign country escaped to a British warship on the high seas, their owner could bring an action against the commander of the ship for harboring the slaves, after notice had been given him. Best said:

> I say there is not any decided case in which the power to maintain an action arising out of the relation of master and slave has been recog-

nised in this country. I am aware of the case in Levinz, but there the question was never decided, and if it had, in the case of *Smith v. Gould,* the whole Court declared that the opinion there expressed is not law. And the same had before been said by Lord Holt in the case of *Chamberlain v. Harvey* (1 Ld. Raym. 146). The case of *Smith v. Brown and Cooper* has been misunderstood. It has been supposed to establish the position, that an action may be maintained here for the price of a negro, provided the sale took place in a country where negroes were saleable by law. But that point was not decided. The Court only held, that the question could not be agitated unless that fact was averred on the face of the declaration. In this case the slaves belonged to the subject of a foreign State. The plaintiff, therefore, must recover here upon what is called the comitas inter communitates; but it is a maxim, that that cannot prevail in any case where it violates the law of our own country, the law of nature, or the law of God. The proceedings in our Courts are founded upon the law of England, and that law is again founded upon the law of nature and the revealed law of God. If the right sought to be enforced is inconsistent with either of these, the English municipal Courts cannot recognise it. I take it, that that principle is acknowledged by the laws of all Europe. It appears to have been recognised by the French Courts in the celebrated case alluded to by Mr. Hargrave in his argument in *Sommersett's case*. Mr. Justice Blackstone in his Commentaries, vol. i, p. 42, says, "Upon the law of nature and the law of revelation, depend all human laws; that is to say, no human law should be suffered to contradict these." Now if it can be shewn that slavery is against the law of nature and the law of God, it cannot be recognised in our Courts. In vol. i, p. 424, the same writer says, "The law of England abhors, and will not endure the existence of slavery within this nation;" and he afterwards says, that "a slave or negro, the instant he lands in England, becomes a freeman, that is, the law will protect him in the enjoyment of his person and his property. Yet, with regard to any right which the master may have lawfully acquired to the perpetual service of John or Thomas, this will remain exactly in the same state as before;" and then, after some other observations which it is unnecessary to notice, he says, "Whatever service the heathen negro owed of right to his master, by general, not by local law, the same (whatever it be) is he bound to render when brought to England and made a Christian." Whatever service he owed by the local law, is got rid of the moment he got out of the local limits. Now what service can we owe by the general law? Service to our country, service to our relations for the protection they have afforded us, and service by compact. A state of slavery excludes all possibility of a right to service arising by either of these means. A slave has no country, he is not reared by or for his parents, or for his own benefit, but for that of his master, he is incapable of compact. We have the authority of the civil law for saying that slavery is against the rights of nature, Inst. lib. 1, tit. 3, s. 2. The Legislature of this country has given judgment upon the question. They have abolished the trade in slaves, they have even bought up at a great price the right of other countries to carry it on. We might, perhaps, have called upon them to abandon the traffic without remuneration. It might have been glorious thus to put down an usurpation against the rights of nature, but we had participated too largely in the iniquitous traffic to be justified in throwing the first stone, and may be considered as having paid this sum as a sin-offering for our transgressions. In *Sommersett's case* (20 Howell's St. T. 79), Lord Mansfield observes, "The difficulty of adopting the relation without adopting it in all its consequences, is indeed extreme, and yet many of those consequences are absolutely contrary to the municipal law of England. We have no authority to regulate the conditions in which law shall operate." Sommersett was discharged. He might then have maintained an action against those who had detained him; and if that be so, how can any action be maintained against these defendants for not assisting in the detention of these men? The places where the transaction took place was, with respect to this question, the same as the soil of England. Had the defendants detained these men on board their ships near the coast of England, a writ of habeas corpus would have set them at liberty. How then can an action be maintained against these gallant officers for doing that of their own accord which, by process of law in a British Court of Justice, they might have been compelled to do? I have before adverted to the narrower ground upon which this case might have been decided, but if slavery be recognised by any law prevailing in East Florida, the operation of that law is local. It is an antichristian law, and one which violates the rights of nature, and therefore ought not to be recognised here. For these reasons I am of opinion, that our judgment must be for the defendants.[14]

Best takes *Somerset's* case, which is discussed in chapter 5, as holding that English law would not recognize the existence of slavery within the nation. That approach would by itself justify Best's judgment. But what interests us is his argument that is paraphrased in Story's words that "comity cannot prevail in cases, where it violates the law of our own country, or the law of God." Best's argument is precisely that the law of England is founded upon the law of nature and the revealed law of God. Slavery is, he holds, contrary to the law of nature, with civilian authority from Justinian's *Institutes* 1.3.2. Hence, it cannot be part of English law.[15]

Best's ruling that what is contrary to the law of nature is not to be recognized by foreign courts is a very rigorous one, and is very close to Huber's doctrine that what is contrary to the *ius gentium* is not to be recognized elsewhere.[16] It certainly does not justify Story's conclusion that contracts against good morals or religion are to be deemed nullities elsewhere.

3 Explanation

hy, it is time to ask, did Story act as he did? That is the subject of the present chapter. The purpose of the next chapter will be to show that the law on the scope of comity was perhaps not settled in 1834; or, insofar as it was, certainly not in the way that appealed to Story. If Story had a choice on the precedents, and perhaps he did, the choice certainly did not exclude following Huber. That point will also to some extent emerge incidentally from the present discussion.

It would be tempting to suggest that Story was being devious or deliberately innovative: that he had a fixed idea as to what the law of comity ought to be but felt bound, in order to prevail, to present his view erroneously as that of the great authority, Huber. The truth, however, seems to be at the same time more banal, and more revealing for the nature of legal change. The doctrine of comity in conflict of laws in the United States rested on a series of misunderstandings, by no means all of which can be attributed to Story. To see the individual links in this chain it is easiest to work mainly backward in time.

James Kent, who had ceased to be chancellor of the New York Court of Chancery in 1823, published the second volume of the first edition of his celebrated *Commentaries on American Law* in 1827, and a second edition in 1832. It is only in this second volume of this second edition that conflicts issues, relevant to us, really surface. In his first edition the relevant treatment of conflict of laws is confused and short, and, indeed, is only incidentally about conflicts. He refers to Justinian's *Insti-*

tutes 1.2.2, which is not to the point, and to the French jurist C. B. M. Toullier (1752–1835), whom he misunderstands.[1] His treatment in the second edition is vastly different—much fuller and much less confused. Huber does not appear in the first edition, but in the second edition he is given pride of place as *the* authority for conflict of laws but, just as Story did later, so does Kent misstate Huber's theory of comity. Kent writes:

> The doctrine of the *lex loci* is replete with subtle distinctions and embarrassing questions, which have exercised the skill and learning of the earlier and most distinguished civilians of the Italian, French, Dutch, and German schools, in their discussions on highly important topics of international law. These topics were almost unknown in the English courts, prior to the time of Lord Hardwicke and Lord Mansfield; and the English lawyers seem generally to have been strangers to the discussions on foreign law by the celebrated jurists in continental Europe. When the subject was introduced in Westminster Hall, the only work which attracted attention was the tract in Huber, entitled De Conflictu Legum, and which formed only a brief chapter in his voluminous Prelections on the Roman Law; and yet it appears that the very great diversity of laws and usages in the cities, provinces, and states of Germany, Holland, and France had produced far more laborious investigations on the subject.[2]
>
> There is no doubt of the truth of the general proposition, that the laws of a country have no binding force beyond its territorial limits; and their authority is admitted in other states, not *ex proprio vigore,* but *ex comitate;* or, in the language of Huberus, *quantenus sine prejudicio indulgentium fieri potest.* Every independent community will judge for itself how far the *comitas inter communitates* is to be permitted to interfere with its domestic interests and policy.[3]

What occurred after the writing of the first edition to persuade Kent that conflicts law deserved, and could properly receive, fuller treatment? The answer is the Louisiana case of *Saul v. His Creditors* of 1827, which was mentioned in the first chapter, and the resultant book by Samuel Livermore, *Dissertations on the Questions Which Arise from the Contrariety of the Positive Laws of Different States and Nations,* which was published the following year in New Orleans.[4] Both the case and the book appear in Kent's footnotes.

Saul was a complicated case involving a number of legal issues and difficulties of choice of law. The basic issue was the ranking of Saul's creditors, including his children, when he had married in Virginia, then moved with his wife to Louisiana, where the couple acquired a great deal of property and the wife died; Louisiana was a community-property state and Virginia was not. Saul's children claimed one-half of the property, as acquests and gains, made by their parents in Louisiana. The creditors claimed that since the marriage took place in Virginia, that law applied and so there was no community in acquests and gains. An abiding impression on reading the case is of the learning or apparent learning of Judge Porter, who gave the opinion of the court. On various issues he cited Spanish statutes such as Las Siete Partidas, the Fuero Real, and Leyes de Toro; the Custom of Burgundy; commentators such as "James of Arena, Gulielmus de Cuneo, Dynus, Raynaldus, Jean Faure, Baldus, Alciat, and Ancharanus, Gregorio Lopez" and others, including Bartolus, Boullenois, D'Argentré, and Rodenburgh. But as we saw from the quotation in the first chapter he seemed to have little respect in this instance for the scholarship. Porter also said: "The argument of this case has shown us, that the vast mass of learning which the research of counsel has furnished, leaves the subject as much enveloped in obscurity and doubt, as it would have appeared to our own understanding, had we been called on to decide, without the knowledge of what others had thought and written upon it."[5] Porter's contempt for the scholarship is real enough, and it emerges that the learning in the case was that of counsel, for the greater part presumably of Livermore, who was on the losing side. The contempt is the more conspicuous in that Porter displays his learning, for which he was noted, also in other cases. Moreover, when he turns to the issue of comity, his discussion is remarkably casual:

> The appellants however contend, that although such may be the construction given to the statute in Spain, that construction is not binding on the court, because this is a question of jurisprudence not peculiar to any distinct nation, but one touching the comity of nations, and embracing doctrines of international law, on which the opinions of writers not living in Spain, are entitled to equal weight with those who professedly treat of her laws.

The strength of the plaintiffs case rests mainly on this proposition, and it is proper to examine it with the attention which its importance in the cause requires.

But though of importance, it is not of any difficulty. By the comity of nations, a rule does certainly exist, that contracts made in other countries, shall be enforced according to the principles of law which govern the contract in the place where it is made. But it also makes a part of the rule, that these contracts should not be enforced to the injury of the state whose aid is required to carry them into effect. It is a corollary flowing from the principle last stated, that where the positive laws of any state, prohibit particular contracts from having effect, according to the rules of the country where they are made, the former should control. Because that prohibition is supposed to be founded on some reason of utility, or policy, advantageous to the country that passes it; which utility, or policy, would be defeated, if foreign laws were permitted to have a superior effect.[6]

For him, surprisingly, the issue of comity presents no difficulty. Comity does not apply with regard to contracts when it would injure the state "whose aid is required to carry them into effect," he says. But the case in no way involved a foreign immoral legal rule or institution, or an attempt to evade jurisdiction. All Porter seems to have meant, as appears also from the passage quoted in chapter 1, is that when the application of the foreign law would be less beneficial to local citizens than the local law would be, then local law prevails. This is to give comity a wider sense than is found in any European writer. In fact it reduces comity to essential meaninglessness. The second half of the passage just cited is in direct conflict with Huber.

Indeed, surprisingly, in the flood of Judge Porter's copious learning, there is not a word about Huber, the main authority on conflicts in Anglo-American jurisprudence. The only Dutch jurist cited is Johannes Voet. To exculpate Porter—but this is only to throw more blame on Kent, Story, and those who followed them—Huber was in his general doctrines of conflicts of law, as we have seen, a "loner." Not only was his view of *comitas* different from that of other Dutch jurists, but also his axioms more or less broke away from the traditional civilian concepts of "personal" and "territorial" law. Louisiana, it should be remembered, regarded itself, and was regarded, as a civilian jurisdiction in contrast to the rest of the United States. Moreover, as a civilian system its roots were in Spanish and French law. Civilian systems varied among themselves in the attention they paid to the jurists of particular schools. Speaking very generally, Italian, Spanish, Portuguese, and French lawyers gave relatively little place to Dutch and German jurists.

But where did Porter get his notion of comity from? There is no indication that he had any real familiarity with Huber though his discussion of the exception is reminiscent. Perhaps he believed he was following the other Dutch jurists, to whose views he is closer. But there is no sign of close attention to them either. Perhaps the most plausible explanation— and it seems to me to be very likely—is that he used a notion or term that he had picked up rather generally from cases that had occurred in U.S. common-law jurisdictions (and which, as we shall see, were based on Huber). Such cases, as are treated in this and the subsequent chapter and are those in question here, do not define comity and seldom reveal the parameters of the notion.

Livermore's *Dissertations*, even more learned than Porter's judgment, is a treatise very much in the civilian mold. But it was written, at least in part, as a riposte to Porter. Livermore claims:

> It having been at least conceded, that foreign laws must be in some instances respected, it has been fashionable, in this country and in England, to impute this to the comity of nations; a phrase, which is grating to the ear, when it proceeds from a court of justice. Comity between nations is to be exercised by those who administer the supreme power. The duty of judges is to administer justice according to law, and to decide between parties litigant according to their rights. When an action is brought upon a foreign contract, it is not from comity, that they receive evidence of the laws of the country where such contract was made, but in order to ascertain in what manner and to what extent the parties have obligated themselves. Comity implies a right to reject; and the consequence of such rejection would probably be a judgment ordering a party to do that, which he had never obligated himself to do. This phrase has not always been harmless in its effects, for I have not unfrequently seen it inspire judges with so great confidence in their own authority; that arrogating to themselves sovereign power, they have

disregarded the foreign law, which ought to have governed their decision, because of some fancied inconvenience, which might result to the citizens of their state.[7]

In his anger at Porter, Livermore rejects comity out of hand, to insist on the absolutely binding nature of foreign rules. He treats comity as including a free right to reject.

But Livermore has a weakness: he scarcely seems to know, and he even seems to despise, Ulrich Huber:

> From the foregoing cursory view of the works of the principal writers upon these questions, it will be seen, that much greater labour has been bestowed upon them, than was generally known to the gentlemen of the legal profession in the United States, or in England. It is not surprising, that we find no dissertations, or treatises, upon the personality, or reality of statutes, among the books of the common law of England. Since the union of the Saxon heptarchy under Egbert, that country has never been divided into independent provinces, governed by separate laws. One system has governed the whole; aliens have not been allowed to hold real estate; and intermarriages with foreigners were quite unfrequent. Questions arising from the collision of opposite laws were therefore rarely presented to the courts of that nation, and did not furnish subjects for discussion. Towards the close of the last century, some few questions, respecting the operation of the laws of different countries upon some contracts, have arisen. These have been decided without much investigation, and principally upon the authority of some rules laid down by *Ulricus Huberus*, a jurisconsult of Friezland. The same observation applies to the courts of the United States; in which it seems to have been the common opinion, that no other person than this writer had ever touched this matter. This author, in his *Prelectiones juris civilis*, has devoted nine pages to this subject, and has laid down some rules, which have certainly not been generally admitted by civilians. He refers to no other authors, except *Rodenburgh* and *John à Sande*; and indeed I should hardly think that he had read the work of *Rodenburgh*. On the other hand, I have not found the observations of *Huberus, de conflictu legum*, referred to by any writer of a later period, with one exception of *Hertius*, who cites his general rules, but not with approbation.[8]

We need not speculate whether Livermore's dismissal of Huber was because Huber was the darling of Anglo-American judges, but it is obvious that he disapproved of the Anglo-American reliance on Huber. There is an irony here. Livermore scarcely knew Huber and he despised him, but he associated him with the doctrine of comity, as that was cavalierly treated by Porter in *Saul*. He insisted that comity (so understood) should not rule the recognition of foreign law and he demanded a much stricter standard with less discretion in the judges. In so doing, he is in large measure coming close to the doctrine of comity espoused by Huber. But the irony is still greater. Livermore's rather crude condemnation of comity, without laying out the limits declared by Huber, gave scope to Story, as we saw in a passage quoted in the first chapter, to attack Livermore and defend the doctrine of comity (though still not in the sense of Huber).

Livermore was rejected, but, then, he was bound to be in the common-law world. As will appear, especially from this and the following chapter, comity in whatever sense the term was used had already become *the* central notion in the strand of Anglo-American conflicts law known as "choice of law"; and also in whatever sense the term was used it was attributed to Huber. Livermore's denial of the worth of the doctrine coupled with his refusal to attribute authority to Huber ensured that his approach would not find favor with scholars such as Kent and Story.

It is thus, in a sense, *Saul*'s case and Livermore's response to it that relegated a close reading and understanding of Huber to a low place first for James Kent and then for Joseph Story.[9] Story was much influenced by Kent. In a letter dated October 27, 1832, thanking Kent for sending him the second edition of his *Commentaries*, Story wrote: "My next labor will be to write a treatise on the Conflict of Laws, in all its branches. This will occupy me all the next year, if I have my health. Should I live to complete, as I hope I may, this much needed labor, I mean to dedicate the work to you, for the best of all reasons, that you will have furnished me more materials than any other mind."[10] Story did, indeed, dedicate his book to Kent; and he cited Kent with approval on comity.[11] Huber remained the great authority for conflicts, but what he actually meant was not closely studied. *Saul v. His Creditors* was so central to Story's thinking that it is cited by him in his *Commentaries* far more often than any other case, despite its provenance in Louisiana.

In addition to *Saul*, Kent cited eight other American cases to support the propositions for which he was quoted above. They are very informative for the state of development, and way of development, of the law. They do involve conflicts law and several of them contain phrases such as "comity of nations," but with one exception about to be discussed, none throws light on the scope of that doctrine. Of these other seven, only two, *Lodge v. Phelps* and *LeRoy v. Crowninshield,* refer to learned foreign authority, including Huber.[12] The selection of these seven cases is entirely arbitrary. As we shall see, especially from chapter 4, there were several others, more explicit, to choose from. Kent's selection is inexplicable except on the basis that he was still not much interested in conflict of laws.

The remaining case, *Greenwood v. Curtis,* 6 Mass. 358 (1810), deserves more attention, since it involves the proposition that a contract made in a foreign place to be performed there and which is valid there, may be enforced in Massachusetts, even if it were void if made there, unless the commonwealth or its citizens would be injured or it would be a pernicious and detestable example. The basic facts were that the defendant purchased a cargo on the coast of Africa, to be paid for in slaves, and having delivered some of the slaves, he acknowledged a balance of cash in his hands to be the property of the plaintiff (from the sale of the merchandise); on the same day he gave a note for the same balance payable in slaves. The action was in *assumpsit* and the verdict was that the defendant was liable on the acknowledgment of the balance of cash on *insimul computassent.*[13]

The contract was valid where it was made; and the judge, Chief Justice Theophilus Parsons, declared that "upon principles of national comity" it might be a legitimate ground of action in the courts of Massachusetts even if it were not valid by the laws of that state.[14] He continued:

> This rule is subject to two exceptions. One is, when the commonwealth or its citizens may be injured by giving legal effect to the contract by a judgment in our courts. Thus a contract for the sale and delivery of merchandise in a state where such sale is not prohibited, may be sued in another state, where such merchandise cannot be lawfully imported. But if the delivery was to be in a state where the importation was interdicted, there the contract could not be sued in the interdicting state, because the giving of legal effect to such a contract would be repugnant to its rights and interest.

Another exception is, when the giving of legal effect to the contract would exhibit to the citizens of the state an example pernicious and detestable. Thus, if a foreign state allows of marriages incestuous by the law of nature, as between parent and child, such marriage could not be allowed to have any validity here. But marriages not naturally unlawful, but prohibited by the law of one state, and not of another, if celebrated where they are not prohibited, would be holden valid in a state where they are not allowed. As, in this state, a marriage between a man and his deceased wife's sister is lawful, but it is not so in some states, such a marriage celebrated here would be held valid in any other state, and the parties entitled to the benefits of the matrimonial contract. Another case may be stated, as within this second exception, in an action on a contract made in a foreign state by a prostitute, to recover the wages of her prostitution. This contract, if lawful where it was made, could not be the legal ground of an action here; for the consideration is confessedly immoral and a judgment in support of it would be pernicious from its example. And perhaps all cases may be considered as within this second exception, which are founded on moral turpitude, in respect either of the consideration or the stipulation.[15]

Neither Huber nor any other learned foreign authority was cited. But Parsons's first exception corresponds to some extent to the wording for the exception in Huber's third axiom. This first exception, Parsons subsequently held, was not relevant to the case.[16] The action therefore had to be maintained by comity unless the agreement fell under Parsons's second exception.

Parsons explains fully what he means by this exception, and where no action would be granted. The illustration of the marriage, valid where it was made but incestuous by the law of nature and thus not to be recognized in Massachusetts, has a counterpart in Huber, as we have seen, though this is not related to the exception of Huber's third axiom. For Huber, the whole theory of conflicts law rests on the *ius gentium*. Marriage within the first degree would be void elsewhere even if valid where celebrated, because it was contrary to the law of nations. Such incestuous marriage is everywhere (else) void, and it is revolting. Huber's reasoning here would also apply to Parsons's second illustration, an action by a prostitute to recover the wages of her prostitution. Such an action is generally barred everywhere. If it were allowed in one place, namely where the prostitute plied her trade, it still would be barred elsewhere as being contrary to the *ius gentium.*

We cannot be absolutely sure from the passage quoted whether Parsons's second exception was meant to be the same as, or no wider than, Huber's discussion of acts or transactions void because contrary to the *ius gentium.* Yet Parsons spoke of "an example pernicious and detestable"; Huber wrote *si exempli nimis sit abominandi,* "if it is a too revolting example." Parsons brought in the law of nature, Huber the law of nations. Not only is the approach similar, but in Huber's time jurists, including Huber himself, regarded *ius naturale* and *ius gentium* as overlapping terms.[17] The similarities between Huber and Parsons here are too close to be coincidental. On the other hand, the views of Parsons and Story on the notion of comity are very different. It certainly appears as though Parsons is following Huber.

But the case before the court involved the purchase of slaves. Would an action on a contract for such a purchase, valid where it was made, be barred under Parsons's second exception? It clearly would not be barred on Huber's approach, since slavery was certainly part of the *ius gentium.* Parsons's attitude is difficult to ascertain. He sidesteps the issue. The plaintiff has the same claim on two scores: the acknowledgment by the defendant of cash in his hands due to the plaintiff; the note for payment of that sum in slaves. Parsons gives judgment for the plaintiff on the first score and, thus, he has no need to decide on the second score. He says:

> The defendant, therefore, to establish his defence, must bring this case within the second exception, and show that the action, as considered by the laws of this commonwealth, is a *turpis causa,* furnishing a pernicious precedent, and so not to be countenanced. This, upon public principles, he is authorized to do, notwithstanding he is a party to all the moral turpitude of the contract.
>
> The argument is, that the transportation of slaves from *Africa* is an immoral and vicious practice, and consequently that any contract to purchase slaves for that purpose is base and dishonest, and cannot be the foundation of an action here within the principle of comity adopted by the common law. This objection may apply to the counts on the note, but not to the count on the *insimul computassent.*

Laying the counts on the note out of the case, we shall consider the objection of moral turpitude, so far as it affects the count on the *insimul computassent;* and we are satisfied that the objection does not apply to the contract averred in this count; there being nothing immoral in the consideration on the plaintiffs part, or in the stipulation made by the defendant. If a *Charleston* merchant should send a cargo of merchandise to *Africa,* for the purpose of there selling it, and with the proceeds to purchase slaves; and if the cargo be accordingly sold, and the purchaser agree to pay for it in slaves; and he afterwards shall refuse or neglect to deliver the slaves, but makes a new agreement with the owner to pay him a sum of money for his cargo, an action can unquestionably, in our opinion, be maintained on this new contract; and the illegal contract, being annulled or void, cannot affect it. So, if the purchaser had delivered a part only of the slaves to the merchant, and afterwards agrees with him to pay the balance in cash, we see no objection to an action to recover this balance in cash, if the purchaser refuse to pay it.[18]

In the last paragraph quoted, Parsons does talk of "the illegal contract," but that is in the context of the defendant's argument and does not indicate that Parsons held the contract for purchase of slaves unenforceable in Massachusetts. Indeed, he expressly leaves the matter open. He goes on to say: "And although, on the same day, the defendant, in consideration of this balance due in cash, promises by his note to discharge it principally in slaves, and the small remainder in cash, yet this promise is no bar to an action by the plaintiff on the account, even if the promise by note is here considered as legal, and *a fortiori* if it is considered as void for its immorality."[19] He claims his judgment would be correct if the promise to pay in slaves was valid, and even more so if it was void, but he does not decide the status of the promise.[20]

The case law cited by Chancellor Kent, thus, had little to say on the nature of the notion of comity with the exception of *Greenwood v. Curtis,* which is at least very close to Huber. The conclusion remains that it was his reading of the case of *Saul* and the book of Livermore that dictated Kent's stance. And Joseph Story proceeded from the position of his friend Kent.[21] He cited him to the effect that conflicts-of-law issues were scarcely known to the English courts before the time of Lord Hardwicke and Lord Mansfield and he referred to Kent—the second edition—on comity with approval.[22] Among the case law Story dealt with in his first two chapters, *Saul v. His Creditors* has pride of place, as it has in his book as a whole.[23] Story dealt with Livermore copiously but almost only to refute him, and to make use of his learning.[24] Story's misstatement of Huber was accidental.

But it might be suggested that this is the wrong approach to an analysis of Story; that it stresses legal culture to explain legal development and ignores social realities; and that practical considerations determined Story's doctrine of comity. Such, indeed, would seem to be the view of Story's biographer, R. Kent Newmyer.[25] While recognizing the important role of Huber (as he sees it) in Story's thinking, Newmyer stresses that "the comity principle in Story's *Conflict* grew directly out of the realities, or more specifically, the disabilities, of American federalism."[26] Would it, then, be plausible to suggest Story deliberately reformulated the notion of comity?[27]

One might begin by asking whether Story's conflict theory was posited on a "State's rights dimension." For a negative response it should be noted that there would in fact be a trade-off for State's rights on either Huber's or Story's approach. For the view that Story accepted, a State could reject the law of another State at will on the ground that it disapproved of it. But then, on the same basis, its own law might be rejected outside of its boundaries. For Huber, a state was legally bound indirectly to give effect to another state's law apart from the restricted exceptions, but then its own law was equally entitled to extraterritorial enforcement. But above all, equally on Huber's view as on that of Story, any state had the legal right to declare (expressly by statute, above all) which foreign rules would be treated as invalid within its territory, or where a local statute was to prevail. Priority then had to be given to the local law.

For Huber's doctrine there is no doubt on this point. By his axioms 1 and 2, law has direct force only within its own territory. Axiom 3 gives law an extraterritorial effect but only indirectly. A state could at any time create law that was intended to prevail in any situation over foreign law that might otherwise be regarded as binding. Statutes to such effect did, in fact, become common in the United States with regard to slavery even before Story published his book.

Only a few of these need be mentioned by way of illustration. The earliest was An Act for the Gradual Abolition of Slavery of Pennsylvania of 1780 (chapter 881). This provided in section 7 in effect that the slaves of persons passing through, or sojourning in the State, and not becoming resident therein remained slaves for six months only, thereafter becoming automatically free.[28]

Article 6, section 1, of the 1818 Constitution of Illinois (which will become particularly relevant in chapter 5) provided:

> Neither slavery nor involuntary servitude shall hereafter be introduced into this State, otherwise than for the punishment of crimes, whereof the party shall have been duly convicted; nor shall any male person, arrived at the age of twenty-one years, nor female person, arrived at the age of eighteen years, be held to serve any person as a servant, under any indenture hereafter made, unless such persons shall enter into such indenture while in a state of perfect freedom, and on a condition of a *bona fide* consideration received or to be received for their service. Nor shall any indenture of any negro or mulatto hereafter made and executed out of this State, or if made in this State, where the term of service exceeds one year, be of the least validity, except those given in cases of apprenticeship.

That this took precedence over the law of other States is made abundantly plain; and the Illinois Constitution was so understood in other States. Thus, for some time (before Story's *Conflict of Laws* and before the *Dred Scott* case) Missouri, a slave State, held that where a slave with the owner's permission sojourned in Illinois so as to establish residence there, he or she became free, and did not become reenslaved on return to a slave State.[29]

Vermont's statute no. 37 of 1858, An Act to Secure Freedom to All Persons within This State, provided at section 6: "Every person who may have been held as a slave, who shall come or be brought or be within this State, with or without the consent of his or her master or mistress, or who shall come or be brought, or be involuntarily, or in any way, in this State, shall be free." This emphatic provision is drafted so all-embracingly that part of it openly offends against the Fugitive Slave Provision of the U.S. Constitution.

But if Story were deliberately manipulating the doctrine of comity it would more likely be toward forming a common law for the United States. It is, indeed, only on the basis that Story believed there could be a common law for the United States, at least in large measure, that one can explain his range of treatises on American law: on bailments (1832), conflict of laws (1834), equity (1836), equity pleading (1838), agency (1839), partnership (1841), bills of exchange (1843), and promissory notes (1845). But one must reject any such explanation for a deliberate manipulation of Huber's comity doctrine. To begin with, it is Huber's comity doctrine, not Story's, that would lead to a common U.S. system of conflict of laws. Second, unless one were to claim that slavery was in the forefront of Story's mind on this matter—and there is no evidence for that—then any explanation that there was deliberate manipulation would have to show that Story felt that his version of comity was preferable throughout the whole field of law. Yet Story's comity made the law much less certain than Huber's did, and I cannot find that it had any particular advantages. And an examination of Story's *Conflict of Laws* shows that slavery occupies very little space. Third, as was argued above, free States that wished non-fugitive slaves who entered or sojourned in their territory to be free could so provide by legislation and this would be wholly consistent also with Huber's thesis.

The slightly different proposition might be advanced that Story deliberately misstated Huber because, though he wanted a federal common law, he believed States would recognize the validity and efficacy of contracts made in other States, and his version of comity would then give States leeway in other matters to reject the law of another State when they regarded it as wrong. This proposition also fails to convince. On Story's doctrine, even the most innocuous commercial contract with an individual could be endangered at the whim of a judge. We have already seen an example in *Saul v. His Creditors*. A doctrine like Story's, but not Huber's, gave the judge the opportunity to decide for himself the law of which State would govern a marriage; this decision could have a big impact on the amount of the husband's property; and this would determine the extent of commercial creditors' claims. Moreover, on Story's doctrine, but again not on Huber's, States would have the right to regard as invalid transactions not involving slaves that were valid where they were made. The most obvious example comes from the fact that in some States, but not in others, marriage with a deceased wife's sister was prohibited.[30] Let us imagine a man marrying his dead wife's sister in the State in which they lived, and in which such a marriage was lawful.

After some time they moved into a State where such a marriage was prohibited, and the issue of the marriage came before the court, perhaps on a question of succession on the death of one spouse. On Huber's version the court would have to find the marriage valid. On Story's version, the judge had a choice, and he could rule the marriage void as incestuous and too revolting an example. Story, indeed, is aware of this difficulty and he claims in this context: "It would be a strong point to put, that a marriage, perfectly valid between such parties in all New England, should be held invalid in Virginia, or England."[31] And in support he draws the common distinction "between marriages incestuous by the law of nature, and such as are incestuous by the positive code of a state." But in places where such a marriage was void—and this was true not only for England and some of its former colonies, but also for some other states, including Holland—this was because of a reading of *Leviticus*, chapters 18 and 20, and hence was regarded as incestuous by the law of God.[32]

Still, we must consider what can be learned from Story himself about the application of his theory of comity to slavery in free States. Two discussions strike me as being especially relevant. The first is from his *Commentaries on the Conflict of Laws*:

> Another case may be put of even a more striking character. Suppose a person to be a slave in his own country, having no personal capacity to contract there, is he upon his removal to a foreign country, where slavery is not tolerated, to be still deemed a slave? If so, then a Greek or Asiatic, held in slavery in Turkey, would, upon his arrival in England, or in Massachusetts, be deemed a slave and be there subject to be treated as mere property, and under the uncontrollable despotic power of his master. The same rule would exist as to Africans and others, held in slavery in foreign countries. We know, how this point has been settled in England. It has been decided, that the law of England abhors, and will not endure the existence of slavery within the nation; and consequently, as soon as a slave lands in England, he becomes *ipso facto* a freeman, and discharged from the state of servitude. Independent of the provisions of the constitution of the United States, for the protection of the rights of masters in regard to domestic fugitive slaves, there is no doubt,

that the same principle pervades the common law of the non slave
holding states in America; that is, foreign slaves would no longer be
deemed such after their removal thither.[33]

A footnote attached at the end refers to four cases that we shall shortly
consider.

The passage is not wholly without ambiguity. Certainly, for Story a
slave brought into a free State from a foreign country by his owner
would become free, but nothing is said about a slave from an American
slave State brought into a free State. For the proposition that a slave becomes free as soon as he sets foot in England, Story cites, among others,
Somerset's case, but he forbears to show any analogy to U.S. States.[34] The
cases cited in Story's footnote at the end of the passage are not helpful
for our purposes. The first is the familiar one of *Saul v. His Creditors,*
which simply relates to the general issue of comity.[35] The second, *In re
Francisco,* relates to the issue of a foreign slave, from Cuba, brought into
a free State, Massachusetts.[36] The remaining two, *Butler v. Hopper* and
Ex parte Simmons, are rather surprising.[37] They are not at all relevant to
the issue but concern the Pennsylvanian statutory rule, which we have
just seen, that slaves brought by their master into the State became free
after a sojourn of six months.

The fact is that in the first edition of his *Commentaries on the Conflict
of Laws*, the one relevant to this question, Story does not say anything
about the effect on an American slave's status when he was brought into
a free State. It is, then, hard to argue that this question was at the forefront of Story's mind causing him to modify the doctrine of comity. In
addition, Story downplays the right of free States to issue legislation like
that we have seen for Pennsylvania, Illinois, and Vermont, which could
have made some slaves free. (It is pertinent to note here for Huber's doctrine of comity that the general rule was that a slave who entered within
the boundaries of the Dutch Republic immediately became free.) [38]

The passage quoted appears with modifications in subsequent editions
of his book, with discussion (and even long quotation) of subsequent
U.S. cases, including those that followed Story's doctrine of comity. But
Story carefully avoids saying how such cases involving slaves ought to
be decided. These later editions, including the sixth from 1865 (edited
by I. F. Redfield), shed no light on the issue that concerns us here.[39]

The second relevant discussion is in Story's U.S. Supreme Court decision in *Prigg v. Pennsylvania* in 1842.[40] The judgment was complex. It held, among several other things, that the federal Fugitive Slave law of 1793 was constitutional and that State laws, such as section 1 of the Act of Assembly of Pennsylvania of 1826, that interfered with the rendition of slaves were unconstitutional. In strong language Story insisted that the power of legislation on the subject was exclusive to the national government. "It is scarcely conceivable that the slaveholding States would have been satisfied with leaving to the legislation of the non-slaveholding States a power of regulation, in the absence of that of Congress, which would or might practically amount to a power to destroy the rights of the owner."[41] The judgment also held that State officials could enforce the federal law of 1793 if they wished but they could not be compelled to do so by the federal government: that would be an infringement of State rights. Much more telling for present purposes was the further holding that masters had a right of recaption without recourse to the courts, provided the capture could be made without a breach of the peace:

> Upon this ground we have not the slightest hesitation in holding that, under and in virtue of the Constitution, the owner of a slave is clothed with entire authority, in every State in the Union, to seize and recapture his slave, whenever he can do it without any breach of the peace or any illegal violence. In this sense and to this extent this clause of the Constitution may properly be said to execute itself, and to require no aid from legislation, State or national.[42]

There is here no ringing antislavery endorsement. Indeed, earlier in his judgment, Story praised the Fugitive Slave clause of the U.S. Constitution, even if only on the basis of "historical necessity": "The clause was, therefore, of the last importance to the safety and security of the southern States, and could not have been surrendered by them without endangering their whole property in slaves. The clause was accordingly adopted into the Constitution by the unanimous consent of the framers of it; a proof at once of its intrinsic and practical necessity."[43] *Prigg v. Pennsylvania* was decided some years after Story published his *Commentaries on the Constitution*, and there is no sign, in his judgment, of any interest in molding the law in an antislavery way. The point I want to make from examining these two discussions of Story is that they render unlikely an idea that Story would have deliberately remodeled the wide-ranging doctrine of comity to enable free States' courts to declare more slaves free, even if the issue had been at the forefront of his mind. Story was strongly opposed to slavery but not enough to base his views on comity on hostility to it.[44] Indeed, while he castigated the immorality of slavery in his judgment in *United States v. The La Jeune Eugénie,* he also stated "It would be unbecoming in me here to assert, that the state of slavery cannot have a legitimate existence, or that it stands condemned by the unequivocal testimony of the law of nations."[45]

All in all, no case can be made for the proposition that Story deliberately misrepresented Huber.[46] No further argument seems necessary but, if one were wanted, there remains a clincher. If one wishes to hold that Story deliberately misstated Huber, then since he was relying here so heavily on Kent, one would have to hold that Kent also deliberately misstated Huber, and that Kent and Story were virtually involved in a conspiracy. But Kent could have had no purpose in deliberately misrepresenting Huber. His treatment is short and nothing is made to depend on it. His treatment of conflicts in the first edition was so woefully poor that he can have had little interest in the subject.[47] Besides, it is apparent that he was taking his understanding of comity from Judge Porter in *Saul v. His Creditors.* And there is no sign in their correspondence that Kent and Story were interested in changing the law on comity. Apart from all other arguments, it is simplest to hold that Story read Kent and assumed he was properly following Huber, and then Story read Huber with insufficient attention.

The main thrust of this chapter has been that rejection of Huber's version of comity came about as a result of a series of misunderstandings. But these, it must be admitted, could not have occurred but for Huber's own treatment of the subject. To begin with, the exceptions to axiom 3 are stated in it in a very general way: the examples explaining the exceptions must be studied before their narrow scope is revealed.[48] Again, he says that no one seems ever to have doubted the validity of his axiom 3; but, as we saw at the end of the first chapter, he was innovating. And he is given to expressing himself about comity in very wide terms, such as that effect is given to foreign law "in consideration of the mutual convenience of nations provided no prejudice results to itself or its citizens which is the basis of this whole doctrine."[49] Such statements are too general to have legal content, but this is only revealed from the examples.

4 Pre-Story

The doctrine of comity, central to the theories of conflicts law of both Huber and Story, relates to all matters involving cross-jurisdictional issues. But as has become evident from the preceding chapter, in the United States the doctrine of comity was eventually to appear at its most vital, with the most dangerous implications for the nation, in situations involving slave law.[1]

In his excellent, informative book *An Imperfect Union: Slavery, Federalism, and Comity*, Paul Finkelman makes a small but revealing mistake.[2] In discussing the "Full Faith and Credit" and "Fugitive Slave" provisions of the U.S. Constitution of 1787 he declared: "These provisions insured that citizens of one state would have political, economic, civil, and procedural legal rights when traveling through, visiting, migrating to, or doing business in other states. Without such provisions, legal relations between the states would have rested on the unenforceable and unpredictable legal theories of the international law of comity or *jus gentium* (law of nations)."[3]

The mistake is that there was no theory of comity, whether in the sense of Huber or that of Story, in the United States in 1787 when the Constitution was drafted. The mistake is revealing in that article IV, section 2, clause 3, of the Constitution demonstrates that the slaveholding states wanted (at least with regard to law applying to slaves) a doctrine that would give the protection to their law that was inherent in Huber's—but not Story's—theory.[4] Moreover, they wanted it so badly that they demanded, and got, the protection of the Constitution for it: "No Person held to Service or Labour in one State, under the Laws thereof, escaping into another, shall, in Consequence of any Law or Regulation therein, be discharged from such Service or Labour, but shall be delivered up on Claim of the Party to whom such Service or Labour may be due."[5] As we saw in the preceding chapter, under Huber's theory of conflict of laws, by axioms 1 and 2, any sovereign territory could declare in law that particular rules of law of another sovereign territory would have no recognition within its boundaries, and the direct application of axioms 1 and 2 would prevail over the indirect application of axiom 3. Without Constitutional protection, even on Huber's view, any free State would have been able to enact that a slave fleeing into its territory became free. Such a law would be valid and binding within its own territory. Within the State from which the slave fled, that foreign law could also have an impact, unless it provided to the contrary.

This clause 3, like other provisions of the Constitution, was apparently part of a deal, this time with machinery constructed primarily by Connecticut and South Carolina. In return for the Deep South's accepting that navigation acts could be passed by a simple majority in Congress —in contrast to the maverick South Carolinian Charles Pinckney's resolution requiring a two-thirds majority—northern States accepted the Fugitive Slave provision.[6]

But Huber's doctrine of comity was not in contemplation. Not only is the Frisian jurist not mentioned, and no term akin to "comity of nations" is used, in the discussions, but the clause of the Constitution was woefully inadequate to give the slave States what they needed.[7] But they could have obtained what they needed by having a Huber comity clause, whether restricted to slavery or not, inserted into the Constitution. What the enacted clause failed to cover but which would have been covered by a comity clause was precisely the situation where an owner from a slave State brought a slave into a free State, and that State declared the slave free and prohibited the owner from taking him back to a slave State. By the Constitution a free State was bound to deliver up to the owner a *runaway* slave, but a State might by statute intentionally deprive the owner of a slave whom he had voluntarily brought with him into the free State.

This, no doubt, would involve a State's deliberately misinterpreting the Constitution. If by the Constitution runaway slaves had to be returned to the owner, how could a State take from an owner slaves he had brought with him? And the interpretation was one not foreseen when that document was drafted. It is plausible to suggest, given the South's success with the Fugitive Slave provision, that they would have been able to obtain a rather wider provision protecting the rights of an owner who brought a slave into a free State for a limited time. Insofar as it could be said at the time that the South got the best deal it could with regard to slavery, this is because this issue was overlooked.[8]

But if, when Story was writing in 1834, there were, as has been estimated, only about five hundred Anglo-American cases for the whole of conflicts law, there were far, far fewer in 1787.[9] How was the law to develop? By cases, assuredly. But then in the fundamental cases the judges had no reliable precedents.[10] One English case, admittedly rather early but very revealing and typical, from 1706, *Smith v. Brown and Cooper,* may be cited to illustrate how issues of jurisdiction hindered the development of conflict of laws.[11] The report reads:

> The plaintiff declared in an *indebitatus assumpsit* for 20l. for a negro sold by the plaintiff to the defendant, viz. *in parochia Beatae Mariae de Arcubus in warda de Cheape,* and verdict for the plaintiff; and, on motion in arrest of judgment, Holt, C.J. held, that as soon as a negro comes into England, he becomes free: one may be a villein in England, but not a slave. *Et per Powell, J.* In a villein the owner has a property, but it is an inheritance; in a ward he has a property, but it is a chattel real; the law took no notice of a negro. Holt, C.J. You should have averred in the declaration that the sale was in Virginia, and, by the laws of that country, negroes are saleable; for the laws of England do not extend to Virginia, being a conquered country their law is what the King pleases; and we cannot take notice of it but as set forth; therefore he directed the plaintiff should amend, and the declaration should be made, that the defendant was indebted to the plaintiff for a negro sold here at London, but that the said negro at the time of sale was in Virginia, and that negroes, by the laws and statutes of Virginia, are saleable as chattels. Then the Attorney-General coming in, said, they were inheritances, and transferrable by deed, and not without: and nothing was done.

To found jurisdiction for the English court, the pleadings had to claim that the contract was made in England, in the ward of Cheap. But then there was a problem. As Holt said (though with doubtful justification), "as soon as a negro comes into England, he becomes free." So for Holt the sale would be void, since there could not be a sale of a free man. Holt suggested that the pleadings should have stated that the sale was in Virginia where blacks were saleable. But then he realized his mistake; if the pleadings revealed the contract was made in Virginia, the court would have no jurisdiction. So he proposed instead that the pleadings should state that the contract was made in London, but the subject matter was in Virginia. Fictions of this type might be useful to get a case before an English court, but used in this way they could scarcely produce a principle such as that the law of a contract was that of the place where it was made.[12] A further hindrance to development was that mercantile cases were judged by the law maritime. Although common-law courts were beginning to compete for jurisdiction by the end of the sixteenth century, it was only in 1775 in *Holman v. Johnson* that Lord Mansfield declared there was a duty to give effect to foreign law.[13]

What was to be done? The standard approach that was taken is set out expressly in 1817 for one major area of law in the English case of *Potinger v. Wightman* by the Master of the Rolls, Sir William Grant.[14] He said: "On the subject of domicile, there is so little to be found in our own law that we are obliged to resort to the writings of foreign jurists for the decision of most of the questions that arise concerning it."[15] This approach appears over and over again.

Numerous continental authorities were cited in that case, including Johannes Voet, Rodenburgh, Bynkershoek, Denisart, and Pothier. But Ulrich Huber does not appear. In that regard *Potinger* is an exception. In Anglo-American conflicts jurisprudence, Italian medieval and subsequent learning have no place and French jurists are stepchildren; the Dutch jurists, and especially the Frisian Ulrich Huber, dominate the scene.

It is worthy of remark, though, that the first reference to Huber in the English reports is by Lord Mansfield in 1760 in *Robinson v. Bland*.[16] Yet, it is plausible to suggest that Huber was cited in the English courts before this. He had been cited in Scottish cases with approval on comity from as early as *Goddart v. Sir John Swynton* in 1713, six years after the union with England.[17] That case then came before the House of Lords in 1715 on appeal, and though the report does not say so, it seems likely that Huber (and à Sande) were prominent in the written pleadings. Moreover, between 1736 and 1756 there were five reported cases from

Scotland involving points of conflicts law before the House of Lords, and Mansfield (who became lord chief justice in the latter year) appeared as counsel in every one of them.[18] Mansfield's predilection for Huber in this area is one of the themes of this book.

The authority of Huber is impressive. It is not just that special prominence was given to him when in 1797—ten years after the Constitution—Alexander James Dallas, the reporter of the U.S. Supreme Court, paid Huber the honor, never repeated in this country for other scholars of the subject, of translating the relevant chapter, and inserting it into the reports of the Supreme Court.[19] The translation, he said, was made "for, and read in this cause; and I am persuaded, that its insertion here will be approved by the profession." Remarkably and significantly, Dallas's translation was reprinted in 1831 in the first (and only) volume of the *Carolina Law Journal.*[20] Even more to the point, as early as 1760 Lord Mansfield was citing Huber—and Huber alone among European scholars—with approval on comity; and it is comity which is, indeed, our main concern.[21]

More strikingly, given the trauma of the Boston Tea Party of 1773, is a statement in 1775 in *Holman v. Johnson.*[22] Mansfield cited Huber and followed his proposition of law. He said, "I entirely agree with him." The relevant passage in Huber is from his *Praelectiones* 2.1.3.5, which reads:

> What we have said about wills also applies to *inter vivos* acts. Provided contracts are made in accordance with the law of the place in which they are entered into, they will be upheld everywhere, in court and out of court, even where, made in that way, they would not be valid. For example: in a certain place particular kinds of merchandise are prohibited. If they are sold there, the contract is void. But if the same merchandise is sold elsewhere where it is not forbidden, and an action is brought on that contract where the prohibition is in force, the purchaser will be condemned: because the contract there was valid from the beginning. But if the merchandise sold were to be delivered in another place where they were prohibited, the purchaser would not be condemned; because it would be contrary to the law and convenience of the state which prohibited the merchandise, in accordance with the limitation of the third axiom. On the other hand, if the merchandise were secretly sold in a place where they were prohibited, the sale would be void from

the beginning, nor would it give rise to an action, in whatever place it was initiated, to compel delivery: for if, having got delivery, the buyer refused to pay the price he would be bound, not by the contract but by the fact of delivery insofar as he would be enriched by the loss of another.[23]

At the root of *Holman v. Johnson* was the fact that in England the sale of tea on which duty was not paid was prohibited. Mansfield quoted Huber's general case in his *Praelectiones* 2.1.3.5 and gave as a translation adapted to the particular case:

> In England, tea, which has not paid duty, is prohibited; and if sold there the contract is null and void. But if sold and delivered at a place where it is not prohibited, as at Dunkirk, and an action is brought for the price of it in England, the buyer shall be condemned to pay the price; because the original contract was good and valid. . . . But if the goods were to be delivered in England, where they are prohibited; the contract is void, and the buyer shall not be liable in an action for the price, because it would be an inconvenience and prejudice to the State if such an action could be maintained.

And he held it to be irrelevant that the point of the transaction was that the tea was to be smuggled into England. The case is decided very much in accordance with Huber's axiom 3 and its exception.

This last point must be stressed. Huber said with regard to his exception: "If the rulers of another people would thereby suffer a serious inconvenience they would not be bound to give effect to such acts and transactions."[24] This was, as we know, interpreted by him very strictly. And so it was by Mansfield. The rulers of England would suffer "a serious inconvenience," one might think, if duty was not paid on tea. And deliberate avoidance of paying duty on tea was at the root of the transaction. But for Huber, as for Mansfield, the contract was valid. Nothing could better illustrate Mansfield's complete adoption of Huber on comity.[25] Again, Mansfield's reasoning is in conflict with the passages quoted from Story.[26]

Mansfield's prestige did, of course, play a role in promoting the authority of Huber. This emerges no more clearly than in the 1808 Pennsylvania case of *Denesbats v. Berquier,* a conflicts case on the law relevant to personal property under a will.[27] It was argued by the plaintiff that Huber, whose authority was against him, "is spoken of with little respect in 1. Collec. Jurid. 116."[28] Of course, then, for the defendant, Huber was the strongest authority—and Dallas's translation was cited—though Vattel was also brought in. Counsel for the defendant claimed, really talking about Huber, "The precise question has perhaps never been litigated in England; but the opinions of learned men whose writings are respected by all the world, and are received as authority on this subject as a branch of the law of nations, are conclusive of the point."[29] One judge, Jasper Yeates, then expressly approved Emer de Vattel and Huber: "It has been said that Sir James Marriott has spoken lightly of the *pra-elections* of Huber; but it is well known that Lord Mansfield has cited his work with approbation."[30]

Huber's preeminence in conflicts of laws in Anglo-American jurisprudence was already established. In a learned British case of 1792, *Hog v. Lashley,* in which Johannes Voet, Vattel, Grotius, and Pufendorf were also cited, counsel argued: "This, which is fairly to be inferred from the opinions of Voet, is distinctly laid down by Huber, an eminent Dutch lawyer. . . . It might also be supposed, that this opinion was given upon this very case, and will decide it, as far at least as the opinions of foreign lawyers can have any weight."[31]

For the United States one might single out for special attention the note of the reporter of *Andrews v. Herriot* in 1828.[32] On the issue of *lex loci* or *lex fori* he said: "This subject in itself deserves a treatise, but I can do nothing more here than to arrange and refer to the authorities, giving the substance of some of them. Huberus, in his title *De Conflictu Legum,* has broken the ground most effectually, I believe, of all the European writers; but even yet, it must be considered as but little more than broken for the use of the American student."[33] He also observed that Huber was much appreciated by Lord Mansfield and Mr. Hargrave (a counsel in *Somerset*'s case). Indeed, in an earlier New York case of 1817, it was even claimed in argument that Huber had invented the distinction between the *lex fori* and the *lex loci contractus.*[34]

Another striking case in this regard is *Lewis v. Fullerson,* heard in Virginia in 1821.[35] It was held in the case that a slave going from Virginia to Ohio with the consent of his owner, who retained the intention to return, did not acquire in Virginia the right of freedom; and that a deed of emancipation executed in Ohio but which concerned Virginia was void unless recorded in accordance with the laws of Virginia. It was argued very properly (in Huberian terms).

> The cases in the English authorities are numerous to show, that contracts entered into between British subjects in foreign countries, intended to be executed abroad, will be interpreted neither by the law of the country of the domicile of the parties, nor of that whose tribunals are asked to coerce the fulfilment; but that the lex loci contractus will govern. . . . The principle is familiar, and need not be insisted on. The common law has, in this, adopted the principle of the civil law, contraxisse unusquisque in eo loco intelligitur, in quo ut solveret se obligavit.[36]

And counsel referred to Justinian's *Digest* 44.7.21. The argument was acceptable to the court. Judge Spencer Roane added:

> The lex loci is also to be taken subject to the exception, that it is not to be enforced in another country, when it violates some moral duty, or the policy of that country, or is inconsistent with a positive right secured to a third person or party by the laws of that country, in which it is sought to be enforced. In such a case we are told "magis ius nostrum, quam ius alienum servemus." That third party, in this case, is the commonwealth of Virginia; and her policy and interests are to be attended to. These turn the scale against the lex loci in the present instance. For want of being emancipated agreeably to the provisions of our act on that subject, the duty of supporting the old and infirm slaves would devolve upon the commonwealth.[37]

The Latin quotation is taken from Huber and is correctly attributed to him. What is above all significant in this aspect of the pre-Story case is the very great, if not complete, understanding of Huber's comity. What is in issue is not what I have termed the first exception to Huber's axiom 3. The case does not turn here on prejudice to the power or rights of another state. It relates to the second exception, to what I have called the rights of another state's subject. It is not only that the Latin quotation is taken from the context in section 11, where the rights of subjects are under discussion, but Virginia is expressly termed "that third party in this case." Virginia is looked at, not at all from the point of view of her sovereignty, but of her position as having residual liability if the foreign contract is recognized. Certainly this goes slightly beyond Huber's exception in that the commonwealth is not a subject; and beyond his examples in that the issue is not of precedence between two contracts but of precedence between a contract and residual liability. But the issue is well within the spirit of Huber's axiom and his explanation of it. It relates to the issue of precedence of two conflicting rights where one is secured by the law of a different state or nation.

What is unclear, because the issues are left unexamined, is whether Roane's "when it violates some moral duty, or the policy of that country" corresponds to Huber's claim that a foreign rule opposed to *ius gentium* would not be enforced, and to what I have termed Huber's first exception to his axiom 3. What matters, above all, in this context is Roane's approval of Huber as authority in this field, and an understanding of Huber that was much greater than Story was ever to show.

As chancellor of the New York Court of Chancery, James Kent was also unstinting in his praise of Huber:

> That the succession to, and disposition of, personal property is regulated by the law of the owner's domicile has become a settled principle of international jurisprudence, founded on public convenience and policy. This general principle is amply discussed and illustrated by Huber, under the well known title "De Conflictu Legum;" and that essay is everywhere received as containing a doctrine of universal law. Heineccius (De Testamenti Factione Jure Germanico [On Testamentary Capacity in German Law] §30; Opera, tom 2, 972) cites that treatise, and the same doctrine in Strykius, as the received law in Germany.[38]

Subsequently in the same case Kent referred to Huber and comity and claimed that acceptance of that doctrine "wonderfully increases reciprocal confidence and credit."[39]

In other cases, too, Huber is cited as the sole or main authority.[40] Indeed, his importance on the issue of comity is well brought out in the case of *Greenwood v. Curtis,* discussed in the preceding chapter.

For a proper appreciation of Huber's stature for conflict of laws in the United States before Story's book, we must not ignore a lecture in 1818 by Gulian C. Verplanck, who was later the author of the celebrated *Essay on the Doctrine of Contracts* (New York, 1825). In a discussion of "gross instances of national injustice" he declared: "Almost within our own memory, a learned English judge, (Sir James Marriott), in a formal and laboured opinion, took occasion to sneer at the treatise of Huberus, *De conflictu Legum*, which has settled the law of the greater part of the civilized world on the often litigated points of the *Lex loci contractus*, as 'the dull work of a Dutch schoolmaster, written in the worst Latin and printed on the worst paper he had ever seen.' "[41] Now, as we know, it was not the case that Huber had "settled the law of the greater part of the civilized world," but Verplanck could not have made that claim if that was not the role Huber was seen to have played in the United States.

Before Story there was, thus, a growing conflicts law in the United States and, so far as it existed with regard to choice of law, it was firmly grounded on European scholarship, on Dutch scholarship in particular, and especially on Huber.[42] No doctrine in this area of law was more settled than that of comity; and for comity Huber was the undisputed master. Insofar as there was any settled law on comity, before Story, based on cases, it was the doctrine of Huber.

Indeed, Nadelmann goes so far as to assert (though, I believe, with some exaggeration): "Thus we have abundant proof of the fact that the Dutch theory of *comity* as known from Huber's sketch *de conflictu legum* was 'received' in the United States long before the Story era—not only before Story's Commentaries appeared (1834) but a decade at least before Story was appointed to the Supreme Court (1811)."[43]

By their very nature, cases usually do not set out all the boundaries of a legal doctrine, but it is worth stressing that before *Saul v. His Creditors,* there is no evidence to my knowledge that any common-law judge or jurist misunderstood Huber on comity. Respect for a notion such as comity in a sense close to that of Huber appears also in a number of American cases in which neither that term (nor any similar terms) nor learned European authority appears. The doctrine emerges most clearly inevitably in cases involving slavery, in both free and slave States.

For the former, the Pennsylvania decision in 1821 of *Butler v. Delaplaine* is a good example.[44] No other state was earlier in its opposition to slavery. Part of the issue in the case was whether, if the owner of slaves in Maryland leased a farm there, together with the slaves to cultivate it, and one of the slaves removed to Philadelphia with the consent of the lessee, the slave would be entitled to his freedom to the prejudice of the lessor, his owner. Judge Thomas Duncan expressed himself, in very forceful language, against freedom in this case, even though by section 10 of the Pennsylvania Act for the Abolition of Slavery of 1780 a slave brought into the State and remaining there for six months, who was neither absconding nor a runaway, by that fact became free. He said:

> Though this is a claim of freedom, we are not in favor of liberty to lose sight that this class of people are acknowledged as slaves by the laws of both States. The master has a property in them, and contracts respecting this species of property, are to be construed by the same rules of interpretation, that contracts respecting any other species of property are. . . . It is contended, that every slave brought into this State, and remaining here for six months, unless he is an absconding or runaway slave, became *ipso facto* free, and that whether the party removing him had authority or not, to bring him in. This construction would be a reproach to the framers of the Acts for the abolition of slavery, as it would be an outrage on the property of the citizens of another State, where slavery is tolerated—a confiscation and forfeiture of their rights, without any act done by them in violation of the laws of this State. . . . The Legislature wisely and humanely desirous to abolish gradually slavery in this State, have cautiously preserved the rights of citizens of other States whose slaves *are introduced* into this State without their knowledge.[45]

At another point he states: "The continuing of a sojourner, must be a single, unbroken one, for six months. There may be cases of a fraudulent shuffling backwards and forwards in *Pennsylvania,* and then into *Maryland,* and then back to *Pennsylvania.* This might be in fraud of the law, and would present a different question; but here there is no evasion—no ground even for suspicion of evasion."[46] This corresponds very much to Huber's doctrine of comity. It is the foreign law that is to apply; this is so even where the subject matter concerns slavery (which the legislature is "wisely and humanely" gradually abolishing). A different question would arise, he said, if there had been *fraus legis:* and this is entirely in line with the exception to Huber's axiom 3. On the basis of Huber's doctrine of comity such a decision was inevitable. The outcome *could* have been very different if the Story version had already been current.

For the other side, for a slave State, Virginia, one might cite *Griffith v. Fanny,* of the previous year.[47] Fanny sued Griffith for her freedom in the Superior Court for Wood County. The defendant pleaded Fanny was his slave. The jury found that until shortly before 23 August 1816 Fanny was the slave of Kincheloe. In that month Kincheloe sold Fanny to William Skinner, a resident of Ohio, and received the purchase money. Griffith was present at the sale. On 23 August, Kincheloe executed a bill of absolute sale for Fanny to Griffith, who then was and continued to be a citizen of Virginia. Kincheloe, though he executed this contract, was no party to it, and the agreement was entirely between Skinner and Griffith. At the time the deed was executed, Skinner told Kincheloe he wanted the bill of sale to be to Griffith, since he himself could not own a slave by the laws of Ohio. In 1818 Fanny returned to Virginia and was taken into possession by Griffith on the basis of the bill of sale. The court, and the court on appeal, held that the whole transaction was a fraud to evade the laws of Ohio. Fanny's residence in that State with the consent of Griffith destroyed the relationship of master and slave.

If we analyze the case from the perspective of Huber's comity, then if the contract had been executed in Ohio between two Virginians, to be performed in Virginia, the *lex loci contractus* would have been Virginia, and the law of that state would have applied. But as it was, the real contract was executed in Ohio, between a Virginian and an Ohian, to be performed in Ohio, and so the *lex loci contractus* was Ohio, and the law of Ohio applied. The Virginia court took that approach, and thus held that the Virginian slave, Fanny, was free because of the law of Ohio. It further declared the whole transaction was *fraus legis,* to evade the law of Ohio. This further reason for holding that the proper law of the contract was the law of Ohio precisely corresponds to the exception to Huber's axiom 3.

On the same facts, if the (later) Story doctrine of comity had been applied, the Virginia court *could have* held that it was prejudicial to the interests of the State to apply the law of Ohio which would make Fanny free.[48]

5 Post-Story

In 1828 Samuel Livermore pointed out the particular importance of conflict of laws for the United States. The States each had an independent legislature and, he observed, uniformity of legislation could not be expected. Besides, one State, Louisiana, had a legal system based on principles different from those of English common law.[1] Joseph Story was equally conscious of the importance of the subject. Writing to James John Wilkinson about his book on conflict of laws he records: "We have already twenty-four states in the Union, in which there are already no inconsiderable diversity, both of laws and of institutions. And, in one of them (Louisiana) the Civil Law, the Spanish Law, and the French Law, constitute the basis of its Jurisprudence."[2]

Important though the subject of conflict of laws was, to treat it systematically was almost impossible. The fundamental problem for both Livermore and Story was, as we have seen, that much of the law just did not exist in the cases.[3] A great deal has been made of the difficulty of finding the works of scholars such as Boullenois, D'Argentré, Rodenburgh, Bouhier, and others,[4] but the real problem lay elsewhere. Such foreign scholars were themselves not law for the United States. In any event, they held conflicting opinions. And when Story was writing there were, it has been estimated, only about five hundred cases in England and America touching on conflict of laws.[5] Five hundred cases on a subject so broad and intellectually complex as conflict of laws are not nearly enough to create a system, especially given the multiplicity of American jurisdictions.[6] But a jurist cannot just, in appearance at least, create new law. Law needs authority. Where it was lacking in cases and statutes, Story appeared to create it on the basis of foreign works.

For the future, Story's work itself was the authority on which conflicts law was to rest. As Arthur K. Kuhn put it, "He fashioned the law anew to the needs of the times."[7] Whatever criticism might be made of his *Commentaries*, it was the object of immediate and great praise at home and abroad.[8] More important, it was accepted very rapidly by the courts, in England as well as the United States.[9] The success of Story's work was so obvious and has been so often commented on that it need not be insisted upon here. But its very success is itself an indication that there was insufficient authority in the cases on conflict of laws.

For the United States I wish to single out for discussion one post-Story case from 1837, *Polydore v. Prince*, not just for illustrating the speedy acceptance of Story, but also for its understanding of Huber, for illustrating the complexity of the law of conflicts even on simple facts, for its incidental revelation of the purity of Huber's doctrine and of the theoretical weakness of some other views, and for what it tells of conflicts law before Story.[10]

The facts were simple. Polydore, a slave in Guadelupe, was en route by ship from Guadelupe to Portland, Maine, accompanying his owner's son, when he was assaulted by the ship's captain. Polydore brought suit in Maine. The part of the issue that concerns us is whether Polydore, a slave in Guadelupe, had standing to bring a lawsuit in Maine, with the approval of the owner's son. As a slave he would have no such standing in Guadelupe.

At an early point in his judgment, the district judge, Ashur Ware, gives part of the argument for the captain:

> The argument is, that the institution of personal servitude, however contrary it may be to natural rights, is an institution admitted and acknowledged by the law of nations; that every nation having the exclusive right to regulate its own internal polity, and to determine the personal state or capacity of its members, all other nations are bound by the jus gentium, or by national comity, to take notice of, and recognize this personal status as it would be recognized in the forum of their original domicil, while they remain members of that community; that personal qualities impressed upon them by the law of their original domicil as to their civil capacities, or incapaci-

ties, travel with them wherever they go, until their legal connection with that country is dissolved.[11]

Huber is not mentioned, but the argument is clearly his, and indeed, Huber is cited subsequently in the judgment. By the comity of nations, a state is bound under the *ius gentium* to observe the relevant law of another state. The judge then praises Story:

> The whole subject is examined with all the learning which belongs to it by Mr. Justice Story, in his very learned and profound treatise on the Conflict of Laws (chapter 4). It may there be seen how many curious and perplexing questions may arise out of the conflicting laws of different nations, relating to the state or capacity of persons; questions which must often occur for discussion in the forum, and judicial decision, in an age of such constant intercourse and inter-communication for the purpose of business and pleasure among all civilized and commercial nations as the present. It may also be seen how much diversity and contrariety of opinion exists among the most celebrated and learned jurists on this subject.[12] And that conclusion will be fortified by recurring to our own domestic jurisprudence. It is stated by Mr. Justice Story as one of the rules which appear to be best established by the jurisprudence of this country and England, that personal disqualifications, not arising from the law of nature but from the principles of the positive or customary law of a foreign country, are not generally regarded in other countries where the like disqualifications do not exist. Confl. Laws, 97. It is now fully settled in England, though it was once a doubtful question, that if a minor, who is disqualified from entering into the marriage contract without the consent of his guardian, goes into Scotland, where a minor has that capacity without such consent, and is married conformably to the laws of Scotland, the contract will be held valid and binding by the law of England. Compton v. Bearscroft, Bull. N.P. 115. The same principle is fully established in this country. 2 Kent, Comm. 92, 93; Story, Confl. Laws, 115, 116; Medway v. Needham, 16 Mass. 157; Inhabitants of West Cambridge v. Inhabitants of Lexington, 1 Pick. 506; Putnam v. Putnam, 8 Pick. 433. And though the considerations on which such marriages have been held valid in the domestic forum of the parties,

where there has been a studied evasion of the law of their domicil, is the hardship and the mischief which would arise to society by bastardizing the issue of such marriages, yet it is not the less a distinct recognition of the principle that the legal capacity of a person to do an act depends on the law of the place where the act is done. Huber (De Conflictu Legum, 1–8) denies that the magistrate in the forum of the domicil is bound by the jus gentium to admit the validity of such marriages in direct evasion of the law of the parties' own country, yet no doubt can be entertained that they would be held valid in every other forum.[13]

The last passage quoted is particularly instructive. Ware is about to decide against what he sees as the view of comity beneficial to the respondent, which is that of Huber.

He further emphasizes: "The civil capacities and incapacities with which he is affected by the law of his domicil, cannot avail either for his benefit or to his prejudice, any further than as they are coincident with those recognized by the local law, or as that community may, on principles of national comity, choose to adopt the foreign law."[14] He is deliberately rejecting Huber's theory of comity.

Ware is about to decide that a person who is a slave by the law of the place of his domicile may nonetheless bring an action in his own name in a state where slavery is not recognized, on account of a personal tort committed upon him in that jurisdiction. His legal proposition would seem to be that civil incapacities by which a person is affected by the law of his domicile are recognized by a foreign country with respect to acts done or rights acquired in the place of his domicile, but not (or at least not necessarily) with respect to acts done or rights acquired in another jurisdiction where no such incapacities are recognized. This is not quite Huber's doctrine of personal capacities and incapacities which was set out at the end of chapter 1. For Huber, a person with a particular status in the state of his domicile retains that status when he is in another state, but there he has the rights and duties of any other person who has that status in the latter state. Polydore was a slave in Guadelupe; therefore, Ware's argument from Huber would seem to be on that basis that in Maine his status would be that of a slave in Maine, with the rights and duties of any other slave in Maine. But there were no slaves in Maine, so his rights and duties could not be fixed by reference to that status! What matters is that, above all for Ware, comity in Story's sense was to prevail. Of course, Huber would have taken a different approach; Polydore was a slave in Guadelupe, therefore property, with no standing to sue in Guadelupe. He would remain property in Maine, following the law of Guadelupe, so he would have no right to an action.

The judge's discussion of marriage of English persons, who required parental consent, in Scotland, where no such consent was needed, is to the same point, rejection of Huber. What it most reveals, though, is the purity of Huber's theory, and the cloudiness of English conflicts law. For Huber, such marriages were valid, unless (as was usually the case where the marriage was litigated) they were contracted in Scotland in order to evade the restrictions of English law. In English law, such marriages performed in Scotland were always valid, even despite *fraus legis;* and according to Story this was "upon principles of public policy, with a view to prevent the disastrous consequences to the issue of such a marriage, which would result from the loose state, in which persons so situated would live."[15] Ware's whole discussion of marriage contracted elsewhere is an irrelevancy. For England the law on this subject was an exception and, at that, exceptional for a particular reason. As Story was aware, if two English persons went to Scotland to make any other kind of contract that would be valid there but not in England, and to be performed in England, English law would not recognize the contract. For Huber such a marriage should have been void at English law, but only because of *fraus legis.* And *fraus legis* is not present in the case before the court. Ware treats the English law of marriage as if it were part of a general rule (though he knows it is not) and he seems to be going out of his way to downgrade Huber.

At this point we should stop to ask the obvious question, What practical difference did it make that Story's theory of comity, supposedly based on Huber, was not that propounded by the Frisian? The most obvious answer is that on Huber's theory, the *Dred Scott* case could never have arisen, far less have come before the Supreme Court in 1856! And *Dred Scott v. Sandford* was perhaps the Supreme Court decision that attracted most public attention, debate, and uproar until *Roe v. Wade.*[16]

There were three main issues in the *Dred Scott* case. First, could free blacks be citizens and thus be entitled to sue in the Supreme Court? Second, did the congressional power to govern the territories extend to the exclusion of slaves from them? Third, did *Dred Scott*'s residence in the free state of Illinois so affect his status that, as Chief Justice Roger Taney put it, "he was not again reduced to a state of slavery by being brought back to Missouri"?[17]

We are here concerned with the third issue. The basic facts were as follows. Scott had been born a slave in Virginia in 1795 and came to Missouri with his owner in 1827. The owner died in 1831 and Scott became the property of the owner's daughter, who sold him in Missouri to an army surgeon, John Emerson. Emerson was transferred by the War Department to Illinois in 1834, subsequently to the Wisconsin Territory, and he returned to Missouri in 1838. Scott went with him and returned to Missouri with him. At this stage of our discussion we should ignore English and U.S. precedents and consider the issue only from the perspective of Huber's theory.

We should examine the case from two very different angles. First, we should look at it on the facts as they were. Under the Constitution of Illinois, as we saw, slaves who entered the State, with the owner's permission and established residence, automatically became free.[18] Dred Scott returned (or was returned) to Missouri. The issue then arises as to whether he was reenslaved. Under Huber's doctrine, the Missouri court would have to apply the law of Illinois to decide the question. And then, on this basis, Dred Scott would be free. Such in fact was the holding in a number of Missouri cases, before and also shortly after the publication of Story's *Commentaries*.[19] If Huber's doctrine had remained in place, the law would have been so settled to the effect that Dred Scott was free, that no such case could ever have come before the Supreme Court.

But, second, we should look at the case as if Illinois were one of those free States that had not pronounced that slaves coming into the State would be free. Let us call this fictitious State (that stands for Illinois without article 6, section 1, of its Constitution) Nomecon. We should begin with a stronger issue and put the situation where Scott claimed his freedom before the Nomecon court while he was in the state.

The Nomecon court would first deal with the issue under Huber's third axiom. If the case was not subject to one of the exceptions, it would have to be decided in Nomecon according to the law of Missouri. Scott had been born a slave (in Virginia), lawfully removed to Missouri by his owner, sold lawfully in Missouri to Emerson from whom now his freedom is claimed. The domicile was Missouri, Emerson being sent to Nomecon by the War Department. The transaction the issue turned on was the purchase in Missouri; therefore, that determined the law to be applied in Nomecon. That transaction was valid in Missouri, hence Scott would be the slave of Emerson.

All this follows, of course, only if the transaction did not fall foul of one of Huber's exceptions. The transaction did not "prejudice the power of another state" because that exception applied only where a party had moved out of a territory deliberately to avoid that territory's jurisdiction over the issue in question. Nor did it "prejudice the rights of the citizens of another state" because that exception applied only where what was in issue was the legal priority of two or more transactions. Nomecon had no choice under Huber's axiom 3 but to follow the law of Missouri, and Scott was still a slave.

But could it be argued that on Huber's view as expressed at 2.1.3.8 the law of Missouri could be disallowed on the ground that it was "too revolting"? Again the answer must be in the negative. Huber's axiom 3 rests on the *ius gentium*. Law valid in its own territory is valid everywhere according to his section 8 unless it is so revolting that it is contrary to the law of nations; which means, it is not accepted elsewhere. Slavery was certainly not such a case, since in the United States alone it was accepted in thirteen States. Despite the growing body of opinion in the Western world that slavery should be outlawed, there were still too many slave States in the United States to make possible the argument that, following Huber on the subject of too revolting an example, slavery was contrary to the *ius gentium*. Moreover, the United States itself had recognized and protected the institution of slavery in the Constitution and Fugitive Slave laws. Huber, moreover, as we have seen, argues that the principles of conflict of laws had to be sought in Roman law, and according to Roman law, slavery was emphatically part of the *ius gentium*. Slavery might be, as Justinian's *Institutes* 1.3.2, states, contrary to nature, but as the same passage claims, it is part of the law of nations. Huber also stresses, it will be recalled, that it can scarcely ever be the case that law valid in one place will be contrary to the law of nations.[20]

Thus, if Dred Scott had sought his freedom in Nomecon, under Huber's thesis the applicable law would have been that of Missouri, and he would have remained a slave. But he sought his freedom only after the return to Missouri. How should the Missouri court decide according to Huber?

There are two possible answers, both leading to the same result. One answer is that the Missouri court could hold that there was no event, act, transaction, or happening in Nomecon that would make the law of Nomecon relevant, and that the law of Missouri applied. The other, scarcely plausible, answer is that Dred Scott's time in Nomecon did cause that law to be that which was applicable and hence the Missouri court had to apply the law that would have prevailed in Nomecon. But that law, for Nomecon, was the law of Missouri. We have here the familiar problem known to the students of private international law as "renvoi." Thus, the law to be applied on this answer was again the law of Missouri. And Dred Scott would still be a slave.[21]

But the proposition that has to be argued in this section is not just that if Huber's thesis had been followed, the decision on Dred Scott's status would have been fixed by the law of Missouri, but the more extreme one that that fact would have been so obvious that the issue would not even have been raised, not even in Missouri and certainly not in the Supreme Court.

The case for this proposition is easy to make. As we shall see, especially in the area of slave law, there had been numerous cases involving the doctrine of comity. On Huber's view, the State courts acting *comiter* had no option as to which law they had to apply. And all States would all have to act in the same way. It would take very few cases, and long before *Dred Scott,* for the law to be so obvious that no further case anywhere would be brought. This would be so whether *Dred Scott* had been in a State like Illinois or a State like Nomecon. In contrast, Story's view meant that by the comity of nations each State could decide for itself which law was to be applied. Different results ensued in different jurisdictions. And fresh cases could and did arise, including *Dred Scott.*[22] And in these cases, including *Dred Scott,* Story's views on comity are prominent.[23]

The issue whether Dred Scott had become free in Illinois and thereafter remained so was, of course, only one of three main issues before the Supreme Court, but it was central. If Scott was undoubtedly a slave, the other issues could not be raised. One issue was whether free blacks could be citizens—a term used in more than one sense in the U.S. Constitution and subsequent State legislation—at least to the extent that they could raise suit in the Supreme Court.[24] This issue would have no point in the *Dred Scott* situation if it was settled and obvious that he was a slave. Slaves could have no standing, except in suits for freedom.

The other issue, whether congressional power to govern the territories extended to excluding slaves from them, also could not have arisen for a case like *Dred Scott* on Huber's view if Dred Scott was clearly a slave. Huber did, indeed, accept that an independent state did have the legal right to dictate the law that would apply within it. A government could without doubt legislate that a state of affairs valid elsewhere would have no validity within its boundaries. A free State in the United States could declare that a slave entering its boundaries became free, automatically or subject to conditions. But the fact is that the Missouri Compromise contained no proposition that would, on Huber's thesis, dictate that a state of affairs valid in the State of origin would be legally overturned in the territories.

If Huber's view on comity had been accepted in the United States, and the circumstances had been such that Dred Scott was free, the other issues in the case would either have been no longer relevant, or they would have had no fire.

For the proposition above mentioned that if Huber's view of comity had prevailed, the issue of Dred Scott's freedom could not have arisen because the law would have been fully settled, it is enough to indicate that comity was a central issue in the years following the publication of Story's *Commentaries on the Conflict of Laws.* For that and the concomitant proposition that the law was not settled in 1856 because it was Story's view that prevailed, it is sufficient to look at counsels' arguments in the famous case of *Commonwealth v. Aves,* which was heard only two years after Story published his book.[25]

The issue in *Aves* was whether a citizen of one of the States where slavery was established by law who entered Massachusetts for a temporary purpose, bringing with her a slave as a personal attendant, and who did not acquire domicile in Massachusetts could restrain the slave of her liberty in Massachusetts and then carry her out of Massachusetts against her wishes. The first significant point for us is that comity was prominent in the arguments on both sides of the issue. The second significant point is that counsel on both sides expressly accepted Story's view of comity and reached different conclusions as to what the law was. Of course they could! Because on Story's view of the matter it was up to each State to decide how far recognition should be accorded to other States. Ellis G. Loring put it for the Commonwealth that comity was not to be exercised in doubtful cases. "Comity is practically founded on the consent of nations, and the need which is felt of reciprocal good offices" and was not to apply here.[26] The judge, Lemuel Shaw, accepted that comity could not apply.[27]

In this context it is of some interest that the case that had reversed the trend in Missouri to recognize that a Missouri slave might have become free because of residence in a free State was *Scott (a man of color) v. Emerson,* 15 Mo. 576, in which the plaintiff was Dred Scott himself. It is fascinating that Judge William Scott, who delivered the opinion of the court that Dred Scott was a slave, based himself above all on Story's view of comity, especially in that it gave discretion to the court to accept or not the law of another jurisdiction. It is most revealing that the court's judgment was posited on the failure of other States to recognize the law of Missouri. Judge Scott said:

> An attempt has been made to show, that the comity extended to the laws of other States, is a matter of discretion, to be determined by the courts of that State in which the laws are proposed to be enforced. If it is a matter of discretion, that discretion must be controlled by circumstances. Times now are not as they were when the former decisions on this subject were made. Since then not only individuals but States have been possessed with a dark and fell spirit in relation to slavery, whose gratification is sought in the pursuit of measures, whose inevitable consequence must be the overthrow and destruction of our government. Under such circumstances it does not behoove the State of Missouri to show the least countenance to any measure which might gratify this spirit. She is willing to assume her full responsibility for the existence of slavery within her limits, nor does she seek to share or divide it with others. Although we may, for our own sakes, regret that the avarice and hard-heartedness of the progenitors of those who are now so sensitive on the subject, ever introduced the institution among us, yet we will not go to them to learn law, morality or religion on the subject.[28]

Nothing could demonstrate more clearly that a court's discretion was central in the Story version of comity.

Before Story, Huber was the great, unrivaled if not unchallengeable, authoritative figure in both English and American cases for this choice of law issue for conflict of laws. Comity was the central doctrine in conflict of laws. Huber had his own particular version of the meaning of comity; and on comity it is Huber again who is most often cited with approval in the courts.

No doubt, if Story had stated Huber's doctrine fully and correctly, and had followed him, some judges in free States would have wanted to subvert Huber's doctrine while claiming to accept it. What has to be stressed is that, on the issue of slavery or liberty, that—as we have seen—could just not be done, whether they had recourse to the notion that slavery was too revolting or was contrary to the law of nature. Such judges would have had the stark choice of accepting Huber (and Story who had followed him) or of rejecting him outright, possibly ignoring him in the process.[29]

Story's misreading of Huber on comity, followed by the immediate acceptance of Story and the consequent lack of attention paid to Huber, meant that there never was the great case on comity in which the rigor of Huber's doctrine was examined and set out, and then either followed, or his high authority openly and vigorously flouted. But perhaps there should have been. There is one celebrated, English, case, pre-Story, where the application of Huber's doctrine would have given the opposite result, where Huber's doctrine was well known to the judges, and where Huber was not cited, namely *Somerset v. Stewart* in 1772.[30] *Somerset*'s case does not stand alone as dealing with aspects of slave status in England, but it is agreed among scholars that the law was not previously settled.[31] It also now seems certain that Lord Mansfield's decision, whatever its fame then and subsequently, did not free the slaves in England. The judgment settled only two narrow points: "a master could not seize a slave and remove him from the realm against the slave's will, and a slave could secure a writ of habeas corpus to prevent that removal."[32]

I should like to discuss the issue in two stages, starting with the known facts in each and proceeding to tentative conclusions. For the first stage, the known facts are:

1. Mansfield's decision, which, despite the rhetoric, was probably expressed as narrowly as it could be; and which was contrary to the slave-owning interest.[33]

2. Huber's doctrine of comity, if it had been applied, would have led to the opposite result. Above all, that doctrine would have regulated Somerset's status by the law of his domicile, Jamaica, where he was a

slave. (We have already seen pre-Story cases where United States free State courts held a person was a slave because he was such by the *lex domicilii*.)

3. Huber's doctrine was well known to Mansfield, who, as we have seen, had cited him with full approval.[34] Indeed, to a very considerable extent it was Mansfield who gave Huber's views on conflicts law their authority in England.

From these facts we can deduce that Mansfield was deliberately ignoring Huber in order to reach his decision. The reason for so doing is not clear, but there are two serious possibilities. First, Mansfield may have believed that Huber's doctrine had become so authoritative as the fount of English conflicts law that he, Mansfield, was about to render the wrong decision in law, and he wished to conceal the fact. Second, Mansfield may have believed he was not bound by Huber's doctrine and did not wish to reveal this disagreement, whether because he did not want to shake Huber's authority in general or because to admit the disagreement would have made Mansfield's position more difficult to sustain. In either eventuality, Mansfield's behavior demonstrates the intensity of his desire to find for Somerset.

For the second stage, the known facts are:

1. Mansfield's reluctance to issue a judgment. He ordered five separate hearings and he frequently urged Stewart to render the issue moot by freeing Somerset.[35]

2. Any compromise that would have avoided a judicial resolution would have resulted in Somerset's becoming free.

From this set of facts we can conclude that before he uttered his judgment Mansfield either wanted or expected Somerset to be free.

Scholars frequently stress Mansfield's awareness of the financial implications of his judgment.[36] "The setting 14,000 or 15,000 men at once free loose by a solemn opinion, is much disagreeable in the effects it threatens," he said.[37] And he estimated that fifty pounds sterling per head might not be too high a price. Besides, there would be the shipping loss in carrying slaves to the colonies, and the decline in property values there. Attention to commercial consequences might help to explain the narrowness in which Mansfield's judgment is couched: he does not declare the slave free. But this forces us to address the main issue. If he had followed Huber's doctrine, as probably he should have done in law, and as he did in other cases, then his judgment clearly would have favored the commercial interests. Not only did he not do so, he deliberately avoided discussing Huber, in order to make his judgment less unpalatable. Oldham says: "The state of the law at the time was such that the outcome was not inexorable. When finally forced to decide, Mansfield did so honestly and, it must be acknowledged, courageously."[38] Courageously, yes; honestly, less certainly. Honorably, without doubt.

Mansfield's behavior illuminates his dilemma and his conscience. His rhetoric highlights his abomination of the evils of slavery. Awareness of commercial interests inhibited him from taking the moral high ground at the economic expense of others, probably including persons whom he would know socially in London. He was determined to do justice in the case in front of him—conduct becoming in a judge—leaving it to other people or another time to pass judgment on the central issue. The law was perhaps not inexorably fixed against him, but he was willing to fudge, even to conceal the doctrine of his own favored authority when in this case it would work injustice. Nowhere does Mansfield treat the case as involving doctrines of conflict of laws.

In a spectacular article, "A Corrupt Judge Sets the Pace," David Daube demonstrated that a wicked judge who wishes to give a judgment for a purpose he knows is immoral has to try harder in order to make his decision acceptable.[39] In so doing, he may be so successful that his decision becomes a model. Mansfield's moral judgment deserves to be included in an appendix to that paper.

Any judge who strongly desires a particular result that is against the trend will have to try harder and disguise what he is doing. All the more will this be so when the judge wants the result for personal, corrupt reasons. But equally, a judge will try harder when he passionately desires a judgment for moral reasons and it is *he* who has set the trend which he now wants to overturn or bypass. And it was Mansfield who had given Huber a position of authority in English conflicts law.

Mansfield disguised what he was doing, to get the decision he wanted. It is a mark of his rhetorical skill that the judgment was central, was long regarded as ending slavery in England while in fact it decided only two narrow issues.[40] Moreover, it disguised the absence of legal principle forming his decision. Even more, it was that rhetorical skill that has enabled him to conceal for more than two centuries the weight of authority against him.

Compassion will not, on the one hand, nor inconvenience on the other, be to decide; but the law: in which the difficulty will be principally from the inconvenience on both sides. . . . If the parties will have justice, fiat justitia, ruat coelum, let justice be done whatever the consequence. . . . The state of slavery is of such a nature, that it is incapable of being introduced on any reasons, moral or political; but only positive law, which preserves its force long after the reasons, occasion, and time itself from whence it was created, is erased from memory: it's so odious, that nothing can be suffered to support it, but positive law.[41]

It would be appropriate to end this chapter on Mansfield's high rhetorical note. But in the present context another aspect of the case demands our attention. The attorneys for Somerset's owners did not make proper use of Huber and comity! We can be sure of this because, if they had, Mansfield of necessity would have dealt with the issue in his judgment. Their failure can only be attributed to one of two causes: either they were unaware of the use they could make of Huber, or they had no desire to win for their client. The latter alternative almost certainly can be dismissed. We have, thus, confirmation of the general low standing of conflict of laws in England in 1772.[42]

6 Hypotheses

I have argued at various times in the past that the relationship between law and a society in which it operates is frequently not close. To a considerable extent, it seems to me, law has a life of its own: a life dependent on the culture of the lawmakers and often largely independent of societal conditions.[1] More specifically for present purposes, I have claimed that often a society has little impact on the legal rules it enforces, but frequently the law enforced has a great impact on the society.[2]

So it was with the doctrine of comity in pre–Civil War America. But I should like to proceed with a different emphasis. We know about Story's theory of comity, its acceptance, and what happened afterward. We do not know what would have happened in slightly different circumstances. But that should not prevent us wondering.

Causation in the social and historical sphere, if not in science, is impossible to fathom. One cannot repeat experiments to deduce regularity of pattern. One cannot change one element, and observe a difference in the outcome.

Nevertheless, we may ask questions, and in some instances at least, return a plausible answer. A first question is whether, if Story had correctly stated and accepted the doctrine of Huber on comity, that doctrine would have been accepted. The answer for a variety of reasons very probably ought to be affirmative. To begin with, there was the already preexisting high regard in England and America for the views of Huber on conflict of laws. Again, there was the very high prestige of Story himself: no view of his would be lightly disregarded. Then, there was the absence of strong precedent to the contrary. And there was an impressive number of cases involving comity where Huber was approved. Last, there would have been no reason not to accept the doctrine. Certainly some free States would have wished not to return to slave States those slaves who had entered their territory accompanying their owner, and would have wished to accord them freedom. But this, as we have seen in chapter 1, they could have done without contravening Huber's doctrine of comity, provided only that they made it plain that they rejected the outside law on this point within their territory. This would usually have been done by legislation. The difference this would have made as a result of settling the law is twofold: slave owners would have been put on notice and could have taken precautions to avoid losing their slaves; and the issue of comity would not have been a running sore, constantly in the view of the populace.

A second question to be put is whether, if Story had expressly rejected Huber, setting out his disagreement, his view would have been successful. The answer is much less clear. We must not forget the authority of Huber in Anglo-American conflicts law. Indeed, comity was the central notion, and Huber was treated as the architect of comity. Part of Story's success was undoubtedly due to his apparent acceptance of Huber.[3] At the very least, Huber's short treatment would not have ceased to be read in its entirety with attention even if only in the translation by Dallas embedded in the Supreme Court reports.[4] Story's very opposition to the great, accepted, authority would have ensured that Huber's thesis received careful and respectful regard. Huber's view of comity would have been welcomed in the South. Northern courts would have had little reason to reject it because matters could have been put right from their perspective by legislation.

Moreover, it is my conviction that if Story had understood Huber he would have accepted his theory of comity. There was, to begin with, his general admiration of Huber. Then, Huber had already won very considerable acceptance by the courts. Again, he had no reason not to accept Huber: if he wished that free States should have the right to free slaves brought within their jurisdiction, that, as claimed above, could be brought about by their passing legislation. Finally, there is no evidence that for his attitude to comity Story had slavery in mind.

In history one cannot say: if A is followed by B and C, and A appears to be the *causa causans* or even the *causa sine qua non* of B and C, then if there is D (instead of A) there would be no B and C, but E and F. Above all, how closely the different E and F would correspond to B and C cannot be estimated. But there is a troubling issue for those who wish to have a society's law emerge from its political, social, and economic conditions and to have the impact of the law restricted to the consequences of its emerging from these conditions.

It is widely accepted by historians that one of the consequences of the *Dred Scott* case and the public furor that followed it was that the Illinois senatorial race of 1858 between Stephen A. Douglas and Abraham Lincoln centered solely on slavery, above all on the issues of slavery raised by the decision in *Dred Scott* and the Kansas-Nebraska Act of 1854.[5] It is also widely accepted that Lecompton[6] and *Dred Scott* accounted for much of the Republican gain in the election, even though that party was not victorious. It has recently been authoritatively claimed: "For Lincoln the election was a victory in defeat. He had battled the famous Douglas on at least even terms, clarified the issues between Republicans and northern Democrats more sharply than ever, and emerged as a Republican spokesman of national stature."[7]

Of course, the *Dred Scott* case itself was a consequence of the crisis as well as a cause for increasing it. Douglas was the author of the "popular-sovereignty" doctrine in the Senate that had led to the Kansas-Nebraska Act, and he would have been challenged by the Republicans over slavery precisely on that score. But what matters here is that the *Dred Scott* case gave the issue a popular immediacy that it would not have otherwise had.

On this basis, it would seem very possible that, without *Dred Scott* (which was, as I have said, more immediate than the Kansas-Nebraska Act), Abraham Lincoln would not have been elected president in 1860.[8] The secession of the southern States would seem to be the direct consequence of Lincoln's election.[9] Secession was the immediate cause of the Civil War, whether one believes the war was fought over State sovereignty or for or against slavery. Probably one should not separate the issues.[10]

Legal historians do not much play the "What if?" game. Presumably, they believe that law emerges from the conditions of society. But some other persons love it. What if, when Hitler's troops crossed the bridges into the Rhineland at dawn on 7 March 1935, the French had decided to fight, and with vastly greater numerical strength the French army had blown the small force to pieces? "It could have—and had it, that almost certainly would have been the end of Hitler, after which history might have taken quite a different and brighter turn than it did, for the dictator could not have survived such a fiasco."[11]

There is, as we know, a reluctance (that I share) to play the counter-factual game. But to ignore it is to ignore life. We all play hypotheses every day. Whenever we make a choice in a meaningful way, we weigh the possible effects of making choice A or choice B. We cannot estimate all the consequences of the choice, but the choice has to be made. Should Saddam Hussein be given an ultimatum to withdraw Iraqi troops from Kuwait by 15 January 1991? What will the consequences be if he is? Should the United States insist that that deadline be kept? What will the consequences be if it does? Should France pursue an independent policy? What will the consequences be if it does? Should the United States attempt to block an independent French policy? What will the consequences be if it does?[12] To ignore that the choices are real and have an impact is irresponsible. The issue for the historian is different. He is looking at the situation once the choices have been made. He does not ignore the possibility of choice. He ought to speculate, at least internally, on the possible (but undeterminable) consequences of a different choice.

The simple, but unverifiable, chain of causation that I am suggesting, tongue-in-cheek, is as follows: Ulrich Huber was the main authority on conflict of laws in England and the United States in the early nineteenth century. Joseph Story expressly purported to follow Huber but misrepresented him on the central doctrine of comity. A theory of conflict of laws was vital to the America of the time, but neither Huber's theory nor Story's version was embedded in the society. If Story had followed Huber as he claimed, Huber's version of comity would have been accepted. A case like that of *Dred Scott* could not have arisen on Huber's theory, certainly not so late. Without the furor created by the *Dred Scott* decision, Abraham Lincoln might not have become president. Without Lincoln's presidency, the Civil War might not have occurred when and in the way that it did.

At this simple-minded vision of causation, historians will scoff, and rightly. But there is room for pause. Historians do pay attention to comity and *Dred Scott* in connection with the Civil War. Thus, Paul Finkelman devoted a book to the issue of comity in conflicts cases involving slaves as an antecedent to the Civil War.[13] J. M. McPherson gave eighteen pages to *Dred Scott* and its aftermath in his acclaimed book on the Civil War.[14] Law professors also get involved. In a book significantly intended to introduce foreigners to American law, the current Story Professor of Law at Harvard Law School, A. T. von Mehren, writes with his customary circumspection: "The slavery issue proved to be too complex and difficult for judicial decisions to resolve. Dred Scott's case became a rallying cry for antislavery sentiment in the North; the case played a role in the 1860 election of an antislavery President, Abraham Lincoln. Civil war between the northern and southern states broke out early in 1861."[15] Implicit in this is the claim that somehow *Dred Scott* was among the immediate causes of the Civil War.

One need take only one element, Story's theory of comity, out of the causation equation and replace it with Huber's theory to realize that we do not know what the course of American history would otherwise have been. Tensions would, of course, have existed between slave States and free States, and they would have had to be resolved in some way at some time; almost certainly with violence. Let us even suppose that, given all the other circumstances, a civil war would have been inevitable. For the South to have won, it need only not have lost. Its victory did not require the conquest of the North. But the conquest of the South was a mammoth task, and some northern generals showed a corresponding reluctance to undertake it, especially in the early days of the war. Without Lincoln's astonishing fervor to preserve the union, no matter the cost in American lives, the South might well have won. A northern triumph perhaps required the presidency of Abraham Lincoln.[16]

There is another issue. Historians often write as if they can deduce much about a society from its legal rules. It will have been noticed that that is a view I would contest.[17] To give examples of that view is invidious, but I choose one example because of the celebrity of the author, the general distinction (and enjoyability) of the book, and the palpable falsity of the argument. Simon Schama emphasizes the disconcerting freedom of seventeenth-century Dutch women to show affection publicly to their spouses.[18] And he writes: "At the core of the marriage bond was affection, tenderhearted sentiment, love. Humanists had long held this to be so. Grotius insisted that '*non enim coitus matrimonium fecit sed maritalis affectio*' (Matrimony is made not merely by coitus but by the affection of marriage)."[19] But the quotation is not from Grotius (nor is the substance to be found in him); it is from the Byzantine emperor Justinian I, deriving from classical Roman sources, indeed from the jurist, Ulpian.[20] So, on Schama's argument, it should tell us nothing about Dutch views of marital affection but much about Byzantine and Roman views. But no one, I believe, would claim that marital affection was an especially pronounced feature of Byzantine or Roman life. Schama here is a self-deceiver. He has also mistranslated the Latin. There is nothing in the Latin to correspond to his "merely," and *affectio* in this context does not mean "affection," but "intention." "For it is not coitus that created a marriage, but the intention to be married."[21]

But the aim of this chapter is basically other. It is not to deal with predictions, whether of certainties or of probabilities. Rather, it is to indicate that legal rules once accepted by a society may have enormous consequences. Historians write as if they can evaluate to some extent the impact of Story's view of comity. I wish to show that that view of comity was not embedded in American circumstances or psyche; that it appears to have been a mistake by Story; that, if Huber had been properly characterized, the view given by Story might well not have prevailed; and that, if Huber on comity had prevailed (whether with or without the support of Story), the subsequent history of America might have been different.

Some historians might claim that the Story view of comity did in fact correspond to the American psyche, that no other view of conflict of laws would have been acceptable. To that, one must make a complex response. First, to repeat, if Story had followed Huber's view, States could have passed legislation preferring their local law over that of slave States. This would have caused controversy but avoided flashpoints, like *Dred Scott*, inherent in Story's doctrine. Second, if Huber was to be rejected, perhaps there was no need to bring in any such doctrine as comity at all. Other theories of conflicts were available. But then, one would have to concede that the very idea of comity persisted, with evil consequences, simply because of legal tradition. The tradition could change with concealment the nature of *comitas* but, on this view, one had to pretend to retain it. The legal tradition, thus, still ruled.

7 Thesis

This book grew out of my continuing interest in the nature and course of legal change, and it remains only to set it into the context of my thesis.

In the Western world, governments are, and have been, typically uninterested in lawmaking, especially for private law, provided the peace is kept and tax money rolls in. But law is needed, and in the absence of legislation it will be made by subordinate lawmakers who are, however, not appointed to that task: jurists in ancient Rome, professors in medieval and later continental Europe, judges in England. Since these subordinate lawmakers are not appointed to make law, their powers to do so are in fact limited. They become self-sustaining: a good jurist is one regarded as such by his fellow jurists; a good judge is one acknowledged as such by other judges and leaders of the bar. They establish this position by skill in applying particular methods of reasoning, which vary from place to place, to the legal issues. Jurists and judges require authority for their propositions and judgments. What that authority is comes to be simply what is acceptable as authority within that legal culture. Law develops on this basis, and is, to a considerable extent, autonomous from the society in which it operates.[1]

Conflict of laws fits into this scheme of things. It scarcely appears in the standard Roman legal sources. But when a practical need for it became very apparent in continental Europe in the Middle Ages and later, because of the multiplicity of small states and local customs, governments were not sufficiently interested to lay down rules by legislation.[2]

The task of creating it was left to the professors and other academic jurists. To make it, they followed the legal culture they had adopted for themselves; they looked for, and found, answers in Roman law.[3] Yet, as has been suggested above, there was no system of conflicts law in Rome. But individual texts could be pressed into service: they could be given a general meaning when once they had been particular; they could be used out of context to give a result never intended.

This deformation of Roman law was necessary if law was to develop, especially in a new field. The approach was not regarded as an objectionable practice, and it won favor for the author when it was skillfully done. But, especially because the subject of conflict of laws was so underdeveloped at Rome, scope for imagination was enormous, and the range of views was wider than usual.

There were many scholarly views and, in general, no system for ranking them. Each was authoritative where it prevailed, to the extent that it prevailed.

One view was that of Ulrich Huber. He is wholly in the continental tradition in seeking answers in Roman law, though he freely admitted it did not have a system of conflicts law. In line with other Dutch jurists, he rested the transnational effect of law on comity, reciprocity of nations, but unlike them he insisted that it was self-evident, and from the *ius gentium* of Roman law, that nations act *comiter* to enforce each others' law. In civil-law systems his theory was not much regarded.

For various, especially jurisdictional reasons, conflicts cases did not come before the major English common-law courts to any great extent until the mid-eighteenth century. There was really no conflicts law. But when issues arose, the British government, as is typical, did not legislate.[4] The making of a system of conflicts law was left to the English subordinate lawmakers, the judges. Judges, unlike jurists, cannot build up a theory at once but have to proceed case by case. In doing so, they follow their culture. These English judges had to seek authority, but there was no legislation and, this time, there were no precedents. Still, authority was nonetheless needed, and the judges looked to find it, as they did in comparable situations, in European scholarship. Even for England, borrowing is the name of the legal game. But the mass of European scholarship was overwhelming and the variety of opinion so diverse as to become unhelpful. The practice, in such circumstances, is to restrict one's gaze: in this instance primarily to Dutch jurists, and, above all, to Huber.[5] But the more it became habitual to cite Huber, the more authoritative Huber became and so the more often was it right to rely on him. In exactly this way was Huber also relied upon in the United States. In the United States, too, despite the centrality of conflicts law in a federal nation, there was a striking absence of legislation.

But law, developing in this way by borrowing from foreign sources with little direct input from society, often becomes distorted, sometimes by accident, sometimes by mistranslation, sometimes by a failure to study the foreign authority as a whole.[6] In this instance there was a series of accidents.

In 1827 a case from Louisiana contained a very long discussion by the judge, Porter, of continental authorities for conflict of laws. In this discussion the Dutch jurists (apart from Johannes Voet) do not appear. This is quite proper, especially with regard to Huber, who, as has been said, had little standing in civilian systems, as Louisiana then was. But Porter showed contempt for all this learning and declared he was deciding on the basis of comity, which he took to mean, in a very general way, reciprocity in order to foster good relations. Since comity was accepted in the common-law states, and Huber was the authority most often cited for it, Porter probably took the term "comity" from the common-law cases. But there is no indication that he consulted Huber, whose view on comity actually was very different from that expressed by Porter. The judge's notion of comity was closer to—though still wider than—the view of comity of the other Dutch jurists.

The judgment called forth an angry (and learned) book by Livermore, an attorney on the losing side. He attacked the use of the notion of comity, which he associated (probably also from the common-law cases) with the name of Huber (although there is no real indication that he had studied Huber in depth), whom he clearly and expressly rejected as authority (which, of course, was proper in a civil-law jurisdiction).

Probably on account of that book (though it does not really matter), the Louisiana case and the book itself attracted the attention of common-law scholars, first of James Kent. He approved the notion of comity found in the case, and he attributed the view to Huber, who was the strongest authority in the field in common-law states. The reading and understanding of Huber on comity was downgraded to be replaced by the view of Porter on comity, really because that was believed to be Huber's thesis. Joseph Story accepted the interpretation of his friend

James Kent. Story became *the* authority, and conflicts law in the United States was irredeemably changed.

The early history of conflicts law in the United States was thus determined in its main outline by the legal culture of judges and scholars. There is little sign that general societal values had an impact.

To test the general thesis here put forward, one might ask a further question: Why did the English judges, in their need for authority, turn to the Dutch jurists above all and give greatest weight to Huber?

The answer will cause discomfort to those who believe law is the "spirit of the people" or has a close connection with the economic, political, and social conditions of the society. The answer lies in the Scottish connection. Private international law developed much earlier in Scotland than in England because in the former country there was no jurisdictional bar.[7] Henry Home, Lord Kames, in the chapter on foreign matters in his *Principles of Equity* (1760) draws the distinction. He suggests that the court of chancery should have had jurisdiction in England, and he continues:

> But the court of chancery being at that time in its infancy, and its privilege as to extraordinary matters not clearly unfolded, the courts of common law, by an artifice or fiction, assumed foreign matters to themselves. The cause of action is feigned to have existed in England, and the defendant is not suffered to traverse that allegation. This may be justly considered as an usurpation of the courts of common law upon the court of chancery; which, like most usurpations, has occasioned very irregular consequences. I shall not insist upon the strange irregularity of assuming a jurisdiction upon no better foundation than an absolute falsehood. It is more material to observe, that foreign matters ought to be tried *jure gentium,* and yet that the judges who usurp this jurisdiction have no power to try any cause otherwise than by the common law of England. What can be expected from such inconsistency but injustice in every instance? Lucky it is for Scotland, that chance, perhaps more than good policy, hath appropriated foreign matters to the court of session, where they can be decided on rational principles, without being absurdly fettered as in England by common law.[8]

Perhaps it is not insignificant that the second edition of this work (1767) was dedicated to Lord Mansfield.

From an early date Scots studied law in continental Europe.[9] The War of Independence at the beginning of the fourteenth century closed Oxford and Cambridge to the Scots, and there were no Scottish universities until the fifteenth century. For a time, after its foundation in 1425, the University of Louvain, for instance, was a powerful draw. The Scottish law faculties, once established, languished, and the tradition of going abroad to study continued: mainly to France until the 1570s, and thereafter primarily to the Dutch Republic. Statistics are difficult: not all law students matriculated, some matriculated at more than one university, some may not have remained long. The best figures now (with his detailed *caveat*) are probably those of Robert Feenstra. For the periods that concern us he estimates Scottish law students at Leiden to be 24 for the period 1626–1650, 89 for 1651–1675, 235 for 1676–1700, 187 for 1701–1725, 115 for 1726–1750, 26 for 1751–1775. At Franeker, where Ulrich Huber was law professor, Feenstra gives 2 students for 1661–1670, 10 for 1671–1680, 10 for 1681–1690, 5 for 1691–1700, 2 for 1701–1720, 3 for 1721–1730. Scottish law students at Groningen and Utrecht were comparable in numbers. Feenstra states that for the period 1661–1750, when the total number of candidates admitted to the Scottish Faculty of Advocates was 663, 275, or about two-fifths, are known to have studied in the Netherlands.

Thus, Dutch jurists exercised great influence on Scottish lawyers and judges in the seventeenth and eighteenth centuries. Equally to the point is the fact that students buy books that are recommended by their professors and that are inherent in their tradition. Availability of books is important in shaping the course of legal development. Books that are not available cannot be used and cannot be influential. Scottish public libraries, unlike those in London, became rich in continental, particularly Dutch, law books.[10] James Kent stated:

> A curious fact is mentioned by Mr. Robertson, in his Treatise on the Law of Personal Succession. He says that of the ninety-one continental writers on the subject of the Conflict of Laws, quoted or referred to by the American jurists, Livermore and Story, a large proportion of them was not to be found in the public law libraries in London, but all of them, except six, were to be met with in that admirable repertory of books of law, the library of the faculty of advocates in Edinburgh. Mr. Livermore, while a practising lawyer in

New Orleans, had collected from continental Europe most of those rare works as part of his valuable law library, and which library he bequeathed by will to Harvard University, in Massachusetts.[11]

The extent of the holdings in the Faculty of Advocates library, great though it is, is rather misleading, since such libraries refuse or dispose of many duplicate copies. Much more to the point is the frequency with which one comes across seventeenth-century Dutch legal works in Scottish private libraries.

As an indication of a Scottish connection with Huber and his work I should mention that my own copy of the fourth edition of his *Positiones juris* (Franeker, 1685) (which was formerly in the Minto library) is inscribed *Franequerae 23 Octob: 1685. Empt. fl. 36 viz g b li 16 stirl. ex mandato Authoris professoris miei* (Franeker 23 October 1685. Bought for 36 florins, i.e. 16 pounds sterling, on the instructions of the author, my professor); and below, *Incepi Relegere in feriis 22 Jun. 1686* (I began to reread in the vacation, 22 June 1686). The provenance of the volume plus the translation of the price from Dutch florins into pounds sterling make it very likely that the purchaser was a Scottish student of Huber at Franeker.[12] In contrast, even at the present time the British Library does not seem to have a copy of *Positiones juris*. Again, my edition of Huber's *Praelectiones juris romani et hodierni*, which was also formerly in the Minto library, is dated 1698: the earliest edition in the British Library is dated 1707.[13]

In this field of conflict of laws, Huber was always likely to dominate in a distant, foreign, country where there was a tradition of relying upon Dutch authority. To begin with, in contrast to Paulus Voet, Huber placed his treatment of the subject in an elementary textbook, lectures on the *Digest*; and in a prominent place, at that. This is precisely the kind of book students would buy, take home, and use when needed. Paulus Voet's treatment was in a specialist book on its own, *De statutis eorumque concursu*, and consequently rarely brought back to Scotland. I have found no reference to Paulus Voet in the Scottish cases of the time. Indeed, in the preface to the second edition (1870) of his translation of Savigny's *Conflict of Laws*, William Guthrie claimed this was among the rarest of books on jurisprudence. Then, in contrast to Johannes Voet, Huber's treatment was explicitly on the theme of conflict of laws and was fully developed in one place. Johannes Voet's views have to be gleaned from his discussion of individual substantive topics, such as marriage.

Specifically on conflict of laws Huber does appear prominently in the Scottish cases, as do Johannes Voet and, to a lesser extent, Rodenburgh.[14] On comity Huber is cited with approval as early as 1713 in *Goddart v. Sir John Swynton*.[15] The case of *Nicholas Junquet La Pine v. Creditors of Lord Semple* also suggests that by 1721 Huber's doctrine of comity had won some acceptance in Scotland: "This he did in the only way it was possible, by making out a bond in the form of the country where it was granted; which as it was *ex vi legis* directly effectual there, so *ex comitate* in every other civilized country."[16] Though the wording is not that of Huber, the argument that it is binding everywhere because of comity is to that of Huber, and not Paulus Voet's. The court held that a bond that was null in Scotland (because of its form), but valid in England where it was made, was actionable in Scotland. Huber was also expressly cited with approval on conflict of laws in *Simon Lord Lovat v. James Lord Forbes* (1742), *Randal and Elliot v. Innes* (1768), *Sinclair and Sutherland v. Frazer* (1768) and *Kerr v. Alexander Earl of Home* (1771).[17]

More generally, Huber's overall reputation in the seventeenth century was immense. For example, he is cited with great approval by Sir George Mackenzie in his inaugural address in opening the library of the Faculty of Advocates.[18]

Finally, the main architect of early English conflicts law was Lord Mansfield, who was a Scot.[19] Although he left Scotland when he was fourteen, never to return, he retained his Scottish connections.[20] It was he, more than anyone, who made Huber the authority for conflict of laws. As we have seen, he began this aspect of his career by taking Scottish appeals to the House of Lords. From his earliest cases he was citing Roman and continental sources,[21] for which he was at times much blamed.

Mansfield's library, which was extensive, has not survived, being destroyed along with his house in Bloomsbury Square in the Gordon riots of 1780.[22] But, to judge simply from the numerous continental authors he cites, he clearly owned or had easy access to numerous civilian writers, and, above all, Huber.[23]

The basic conclusions of the book scarcely need to be set down. Important as doctrines of conflict of laws inevitably were in the United

States, given the numerous States, their development would be described by a plain man as "happenstance." They were not planned, nor did they emerge from the psyche of the nation. The central doctrine, that of comity as understood by Huber, was adopted from English law. The English law was developed primarily by Lord Mansfield, who based it on his experience in Scottish appeal cases. Scots law was influenced by Huber because many Scots law students studied at Dutch universities. Huber's view of comity was not highly regarded in civil-law jurisdictions and came to be misunderstood in the United States because of a judgment, praising comity, but not in Huber's sense, from the civilian State of Louisiana. Story's *Commentaries on the Conflict of Laws* was the main vehicle for the acceptance of this different view of comity, but Story had simply misunderstood Huber.

Appendix A   Huber's *Positiones Juris*

T he curious features of this subject seem endless. In this appendix I should like to deal with one further peculiarity from Huber himself. The first edition of his *Positiones juris* appeared in 1682, that is, after volume 1 of his *Praelectiones* (1678), covering Justinian's *Institutes*, and before volumes 2 and 3, covering the *Digest* (1689, 1690). The *Positiones juris*, in effect, is in two parts, the first on the *Institutes*, the latter on the *Digest*. Robert Feenstra describes the *Positiones juris* as a *kort begrip,* a "summary" of the *Praelectiones.*[1] That, though I am not disputing Feenstra's judgment, may be accurate for the portion on the *Institutes* without necessarily being accurate for the portion on the *Digest*.

As one might expect, Huber's treatment of conflicts in the *Positiones juris* appears in the *Digest* section, again on D.1.3, *De legibus, senatus consultis et longa consuetudine* (On laws, decrees of the senate and long usage). The relevant texts read:

> 22. Today, throughout Europe there is a frequent and difficult question: if a transaction has its beginning in one place, its conclusion in another, of which place are the laws, often differing and conflicting, to be observed? We are speaking of different states; in the same state, as was the case with the Romans, once having one Empire, the issue does not exist.
>
> 23. The first and most important rule is: no law has validity beyond its territory, and every law binds those who are found within the territory of the legislator: *D*.2.1.20. This applies even to foreigners: *D*.48.22.7.10, *in fine.*
>
> 24. Hence the form for solemnizing a transaction *inter vivos* or *mortis causa* ought to be furnished according to the formalities of the place in which the act is performed, even by outsiders, and thus it is perfect or not, is valid or is void, in every place: Gail, *book 2, observation 123;* Sande, *book 4, title 1, definition, 14.*[2]

Huber then proceeds to the discussion of which law governs procedure and execution of judgment, contracts, moveable and immoveable property, and personal qualities, just as he does in his *Praelectiones*.

But this is a very primitive account, for Huber. There is no mention of axioms, none of comity, and none of exceptions. Nothing explains the basis for recognizing foreign law. Exactly the wording just given appears in the edition of the *Positiones juris* most relevant for us, the fourth of 1685, published just before his famous account in *Praelectiones* 2.1.3 (1689).[3]

How can this be? We have already seen in chapter 1 his developed notion of comity—though not the word—in *De jure civitatis* 3.10.1, of 1684. And his views of conflicts is well set forth in what has the appearance of a practitioners' manual, *Heedensdaegse Rechtsgeleertheyd*, of 1686. Why is there lacking a short but comprehensive account of the axioms in his elementary text? One explanation, and only one, occurs to me. It is that, despite the subsequent fame of his treatment of conflict of laws, Huber did not attach the same importance to it. This could even account for the brevity of his treatment in the *Praelectiones*.

Appendix B   James Kent's First Edition

I t is important for the argument of the book that James Kent in the second edition of his *Commentaries on American Law* accepted the version of comity found in *Saul v. His Creditors* and attributed it to Huber. Kent was mistaken, because he had little real interest in conflict of laws. The purpose of this appendix is to demonstrate this lack of interest from Kent's first edition. In it, Kent does not deal with the basis of conflict of laws directly: his discussion appears at the beginning of his treatment of sale, where he has a few general pages. At an early point (p. 364) he claims:

> A contract valid by the law of the place where it is made, is valid every where *jure gentium,* and on that broad foundation all contracts were introduced.[a] If it were otherwise, the citizens of one nation could not contract, or carry on commerce in the territories of another. The necessities of commerce require, that acts valid where made, should be recognised in other countries, provided they be not contrary to the independence of nations, and do not proceed from the public power.[b]

His notes are:

> [a]*Inst.* 1.2.2. *ex hoc jure gentium, omnes pene contractus introducti sunt.*
>
> [b]This principle of public law, says *Toullier, Droit Civil,* tome 10.117. is well explained and enforced by *M. Bayard,* in the *Nouvelle Collection de Jurisprudence,* tome 9. p. 759 and which he undertook in conjunction with *M Camus.*

The passage cited from the *Institutes* does not at all justify Kent's proposition that a contract valid where it is made is valid everywhere. Justinian is there distinguishing the law of nature (*ius naturale*), the law of all peoples (*ius gentium*), and the law of a state (*ius civile*), and he declares that *ius gentium* is law common to all people and that contracts arise from this *ius gentium*. There is nothing to justify the deduction from this that a contract valid where it is made is valid everywhere. Even more to the point, Kent has overlooked *pene*, "almost"; that is, the quotation from the *Institutes* says: "from that *ius gentium, almost* all of the contracts were introduced." The point of this is that the earliest Roman contract, *stipulatio,* was at first restricted in its use to citizens, hence it was part of the *ius civile,* not the *ius gentium.*[1] This fact turns Kent's use of the quotation into nonsense. But Kent has taken the Roman text from Toullier at paragraph 79:

> In the contracts made before notaries in foreign lands, the private will of the parties concords with the public power: one forms the obligation, the other makes it executory. In our ordonnance the legislator thus separates the work of the public power from the work of the will of the parties: it destroys the one and preserves the other. He means the obligation not to be executory in France: but at the same time he intends that it have the role of *simple promises.*[2]

At the end of the passage quoted, Toullier has a footnote that begins:

> *Simple promises.* Even when one of the parties is unable to sign, for the law makes no distinction. The authenticated act made before foreign notaries between two parties who do not know how to sign, or of whom only one does not know how to do so, has no less validity in France as a simple promise. This is a principle founded in the law of nations (*ius gentium*) and is established by the unanimous consent of all nations, even tacitly and without an express written treaty, for the common utility of all people: "*through force of circumstances and human necessity*"; J.1.2.2.
>
> "*From this law of nations came almost all the contracts, as sale, hire, partnership, deposit, loan and innumerable others.*"
>
> If it was otherwise, the citizens of one nation could not contract, nor consequently enter into any commerce, in the territory of another nation. It was therefore agreed, "*by the tacit agreement of peoples*" that "if the contracts are clothed in the conditions necessary for authentication in the place where they were made, they carry their authentication in every country in the world." This is a point of doctrine well developed by M. Bayard in the *Nouvelle Collection de Jurisprudence* that he undertook with M. Camus.

Then follows in Toullier a long quotation from Bayard. At paragraphs 77 to 79 Toullier is making a complex point. The French ordonnance of 1629, he claims, drew a distinction with regard to foreign contracts: it sustains them insofar as they depend on the will of the parties, but annuls them in France insofar as they are attached to the foreign power. Thus, with regard to contracts made abroad before notaries, there is a concurrence between the public power and the will of the parties. The public power attributes legal effect to the notarial formalities and renders the agreement executory; the will of the parties creates the obligation. The ordonnance destroys that part of the arrangement that depends on the foreign public power, but it sustains that part that depends on the will of the parties, hence the contract has the force of a simple promise.

Toullier is best understood in terms of a French conception of obligation which was mentioned in chapter 2 and which goes back before the *code civil* but has an impact even thereafter. For Pothier, obligations are imperfect or perfect. An imperfect obligation is a duty owed to no specific person but only to God and which cannot be exacted by any individual. Perfect obligations give those to whom we are bound the right to demand performance. Perfect obligations are of two types: those that form a *vinculum iuris,* a civil obligation that will be enforced in court; and those that form a *solius aequitatis vinculum,* a natural obligation, that gives the promisee the right in the forum of conscience to demand performance.[3] On this analysis, the foreign contract before a notary that is described by Toullier is a perfect natural obligation, thus owed to a specific person but only in the forum of conscience. A perfect natural obligation is not without effect in French law. Thus, a preexisting natural obligation that is followed by an act recognizing it, which, however, is lacking in the formalities needed for a binding civil-law obligation, will create a full civil-law obligation.

But Toullier's footnote is a little odd. The first paragraph is in harmony with his text, but then the quotation from J.1.2.2 is just as irrelevant—even worse—for Toullier as it is for Kent. The remainder of the note quoted here relating to Camus actually contradicts Toullier's own text. In contrast to Toullier, Camus gives the proposition of law that Kent cites Toullier for, namely, that a contract valid where it is made is valid everywhere.

To return to the qualification in the final sentence quoted from Kent: "provided they be not contrary to the independence of nations, and do not proceed from the public power." Though it is not easy to know what Kent precisely means, since he adds nothing in explanation, there would seem to be here a misunderstanding of Toullier. "Proceeding from the public power" seems to refer to Toullier's point about particular formalities established by the law of the land, but Toullier has nothing corresponding to the first part of the qualification. Rather, Kent's own words here indicate that for him the whole qualification is to the effect that a contract made abroad which is the object of foreign political endeavors does not share in the universal validity of foreign-made contracts.

Kent's total misuse and misunderstanding of J.1.2.2 and his faulty use of Toullier are quite inexplicable if he had any real interest in conflict of laws. Besides, if he were really attending to that issue one would have expected him to follow his usual course and cite English and American cases.

Appendix C   The Case of *The Ship Columbus*

I n two places in chapter 4 there is reference to Sir James Marriott's disapprobation of Huber. The reference is to the case of *The Ship Columbus*, in the High Court of Admiralty, 18 December 1789. The High Court of Admiralty (in Doctors Commons) did not have its cases reported, but this one is an exception recorded by Francis Hargrave in the first volume of his *Collectanea juridica*, published in 1791.[1]

Part of the issue was *fraus legis,* evasion of the law which should govern. Marriott in his judgment declared that *fraus legis* was not part of English law:

> However, there is one argument which affects Mr. LeMesurier and the mercantile world, and the constitution of the laws of this country, which merits notice from this court; and the more so, as the argument has been getting into fashion, from a *dictum* of a very venerable character, which turns out only a quotation of a writer not possessing or deserving of celebrity—the *evasion* of the laws! The law of England knows not of any such thing. The law cannot be evaded. The law exists, or does not exist.[2]

The answer begs the question. When there is evasion, when parties subject to a jurisdiction leave it deliberately to effect an act that touches that jurisdiction, the relevant law to be applied will be affected simply because there is evasion.

The "writer not possessing or deserving of celebrity" was, as we shall see, Huber. Further on, Sir James continued in his whimsical way:

> In rummaging the immense piles of foreign learning, and those of Dutch and German schools, published by every graduate on his proceeding to an academical degree, containing all the reading never to be read, a passage was found in the Praelections of Huberus, a Dutch schoolmaster, or, in other words, a professor of a foreign University.

"He says, that the legality of an act done in a foreign country makes, by the general law of nations, and the practice of Europe, an act legal in the proper country of the parties, although it would have been illegal *in foro domestico,* if the thing done had been transacted at home. Thus (says he) a party not being of full age and capable of contracting marriage until twenty-five years old, in the province (I think it is) of Overyssel, leaps over a dyke into the province of ——, where a party is of age at twenty-one, and there solemnizes marriage, and returns back, then such marriage is held good by the law of Overyssel; which (says the learned professor) is very impolitic and ill-judged, because it is dishonourable for any government to give a sanction against itself to the laws of any other country; for that is *in fraudem legis,* a defrauding its own law; and though this act is valid, yet (says the *rector magnificus*) in my *opinion* it *ought not* to be."

Did not the good man see that there is no *fraus legis,* no evasion, no defrauding the law of Overyssel by this act, but that the law of Overyssel is so—If you stay at home, you shall conform to the ancient laws and customs at home; but if you will take the trouble to skip over the next ditch, you shall have the benefit of the leap for your matrimony, and our law on your return holds it valid. Why? Because as a trading, free, and enlightened nation, we know that every marriage is a gain to the state and to true religion, in spite of obsolete laws and restraints, invented by priests for the trade of indulgences, and encouragement of luxury and penance.

The only answer to the opinion is, The decision is worthy of the professor.—I will say no more than that this narrow-minded ridiculous speculation is written in the worst Latin that ever was read, and published on the worst paper that ever was printed.[3]

Sir James had not seen Huber's *Praelectiones!* He has taken his quotation from a student's thesis or disputation, and such were frequently published, even under the name of the professor.[4] Not only is the source of the quotation, in effect, stated explicitly, but the example given in it is not in the *Praelectiones* as concerning Overyssel. And, of course, the law stated as that of Overyssel is not that given by Huber as the law of Friesland.

The treatment has various implications for us. First, we see again how little learning there was in England on conflict of laws even at the end of the eighteenth century. Authority had to be rummaged for: and it was foreign at that. Books, as well as learning, were scarce. Second, the common English distaste for foreign legal authority even when they had no other, is made plain. Third, this highlights again the importance of Lord Mansfield, the Scot, both in developing conflicts law and in giving authority to Huber. Fourth, that this scurrilous passage was relied on by counsel in *Denesbats v. Berquier,* 1 Binn. 336 (Pennsylvania, 1808), in an attempt to discredit Huber is an indication of the standing Huber had in fact achieved. For counsel's case Huber had to be discredited but there was not a better source for disapproval.

One oddity remains. It was accepted in English law—as was clearly brought out by Mansfield in *Holman v. Johnson*, 1 Cowp. 341, that attempted evasion, or *fraus legis*, would affect the determination of which law was to apply. The case of English persons being validly married in Scotland when the marriage would have been void if performed in England was exceptional, but Marriott treats it as the rule.[5]

Appendix D   Story, Beale, and Moveable Property

A s stated in the Introduction, I do not want to take "choice of law" issues beyond *Dred Scott* in this book. But to show that the subsequent history of conflict of laws was just as full of fascination and misunderstanding I should like to call attention to one issue.

Joseph Henry Beale, who had been the reporter for the *Restatement of the Conflict of Laws* for the American Law Institute, stated in 1935: "The maxim *mobilia sequuntur personam* was introduced by Story from certain obscure French authors. It cannot be found in Bartolus' dealing with Conflict of Laws and no trace of it has been found in English or American law before Story. It has proved to be a refuge for a judge in a hurry, confronted with a difficult situation; and indeed like all maxims it serves celerity rather than soundness of thought."[1]

This statement could scarcely be less true. Story supports his view not only with French authority, obscure or not, but also with Johannes Voet, Paulus Voet, Hertius, Bynkershoek, and even Huber himself.[2] It was, in fact, the accepted civil-law position. Bynkershoek, indeed, affirmed that it was so accepted that no one dared to say the contrary. But more to our purpose, it was already established doctrine in the common law that "moveables follow the person."

For England, as early as 1744, in *Pipon v. Pipon*, Ambler 25, Lord Hardwicke was declaring: "If I was to go into the general question, the personal estate follows the person, and becomes distributable according to the law or custom of the place where the intestate lived."[3] Lord Loughborough held in 1791, in *Sill v. Worswick*, 1 H. Black. 665:

> First, it is a clear proposition, not only of the law of England, but of every country of the world, where law has the semblance of science, that personal property has no locality. The meaning of that is, not that personal property has no visible locality, but that it is subject to that law which governs the person of

the owner. With respect to the disposition of it, with respect to the transmission of it, either by succession, or the act of the party, it follows the law of the person.[4]

Chief Justice Charles Abbott declared in 1826 in *Doe v. Vardill*, 5 B. & C. 439: "Personal property has no locality, and even with respect to that it is not correct to say that the law of England gives way to the law of a foreign country, but that it is part of the law of England that personal property should be distributed according to the ius domicilii."[5] Further cases could be, and were by Story, cited to the same effect.[6]

For the United States, pride of place must be given to a judgment of Story himself in 1818 when sitting as a federal circuit justice for the District of Massachusetts: "There are some points in the argument, which may be disposed of in a few words. In the first place the distribution, whether made here or abroad, must be according to the law of the testator's domicile. This, although once a question vexed with much ingenuity and learning in courts of law, is now so completely settled by a series of well considered decisions that it cannot be brought into judicial doubt."[7] This very strong statement is then supported by Story with massive authority from continental and Scottish jurists, and English and American decisions.

An earlier case that might be quoted is *De Sorry v. Terrier de Laistre*, 2 H. & J. 191 (Md., 1807) per Chief Judge Jeremiah Townley Chase: "The court are of opinion, that personal property adheres to the person; that wherever the person is domiciled, the property goes in distribution, according to the laws of that country."[8] Thus, Beale wrongly described an early fixed principle of Anglo-American common law as an invention of Joseph Story.[9] Misrepresentations continued in the history of conflict of laws.

The rule that Beale wanted to use, to replace what he considered was Story's invention, was that moveable, like immoveable, property should be governed by the place where it was situated. This, indeed, was already basically the law in Beale's time.[10]

But how had the law come to be changed between the time of Story and Beale? The full answer to this question would take us well beyond the stated purpose of this book. The short answer is that the change came about primarily as a result of judges responding to Francis Wharton's arguments for it in his *Conflict of Laws*, first published in Philadelphia in 1872.[11] An examination of the relevant pages reveals that Wharton had very few cases to rely on and that these few correspond to the exceptions which one could find even before Story. Thus, for instance, in a Tennessee case of 1860, the owner of slaves was domiciled in Texas, where the period for adverse possession to run was three years, but the slaves were in Tennessee, where only two years was needed for prescription.[12] The court held that after two years of adverse possession in Tennessee prescription was complete, though if the law of the owner's domicile had been the proper approach, three years would have been necessary. But such problems had existed in Story's time and were known to him.[13] Wharton's few cases do not mean that the basic rule *mobilia sequuntur personam* had been changed. In fact, Wharton was not claiming to give the law as it was but as it should be. And, indeed, as it came to be!

But where did Wharton get his idea and arguments from? His treatment leaves no doubt but that he was primarily influenced by Friedrich Carl von Savigny's *System des heutigen römischen Rechts* (*System of Contemporary Roman Law*). The eighth volume of this book, in which Savigny dealt with conflict of laws, appeared in 1849, that is, some time after Story's *Conflicts*.[14] Significantly, from our perspective, a translation into English by W. Guthrie was published in Edinburgh in 1869 with the title, *A Treatise on the Conflict of Laws by F. K. von Savigny*.

The acceptance of the proposition that moveables are governed by the law of the place where they are situated is, thus, another example where American law in the nineteenth century was profoundly influenced by the work of a civilian jurist.

Appendix E   Doctrinal Legal History

octrinal legal history is unfashionable in the United States. Indeed, for the American Society of Legal History's meeting in San Francisco in September 1991, a scheduled panel discussion is entitled "Doctrinal Legal History: Everybody's Favorite Whipping Boy." But this book is about doctrinal legal history, and I hope I have shown that an understanding of American law is impossible without a history of legal doctrine. The book is restricted to one aspect of conflict of laws, but the message can be generalized: for the United States in the nineteenth century, a history of, say, contract or torts is bound to be misleading if legal doctrine is ignored or downplayed.

Yet I must end on a pessimistic note. It is, to me, inconceivable that many scholars of American law will pay attention to the importance of doctrine for legal history. This is not because doctrine is unimportant or because, as some believe, societal concerns determine legal outcomes. Rather, the scholars do not have the tools for the job; hence they believe the job cannot be worth doing.

The problem is that to understand doctrinal legal history one has to look at judicial decisions and juristic discussions from the legal cultural standpoint of the participants. Accordingly, one has to range over materials from many countries and centuries. The participants themselves, it should be noted, will often be unaware of the parameters of their cultural heritage.

A few examples from this small book will illuminate the scope of the problem. To understand the role attributed by Huber to axioms, one has to read his *Positiones juris* and the first volume of his *Praelectiones juris romani et hodierni*, which were never translated from Latin into English and which are not cited in the literature or cases on conflict of laws. If one does not know the meaning of "axiom" for Huber, one runs the risk of failing to treat his axiom 3 as a binding rule. To appreciate the legal basis for Huber of his three axioms, one must know how medieval and later jurists deliberately misused Roman legal texts to construct new law. One must know enough Roman law to understand the meaning of *ius gentium* as the basis for Huber's axiom 3 when there were no textual sources for his proposition: and one must keep that meaning apart from the current sense of the phrase as "international law." Only then, moreover, can one see why Story misunderstood Huber on the point.

To comprehend the approach to comity by Judge Porter in *Saul v. His Creditors* and by Livermore in his book, one must appreciate the far greater importance attached to jurists other than Huber for conflict of laws in civil-law systems. Kent's easy acceptance of the mistaken, *Saul*, version of comity in his second edition can be fully understood only when one is conscious of Kent's inadequate treatment in the first edition. That that treatment is woefully inadequate will be noticed only by someone who can understand Kent's misuse and misunderstanding of Justinian's *Institutes*, and his misunderstanding of the relevant passage of Toullier's book, which was never translated from the French into English. The misunderstanding can be explained only by someone aware of the continental distinction between a perfect obligation and an imperfect obligation; and this awareness is also necessary if one wants to understand Story's response to Livermore on comity.

The central role of Huber in the United States for this subject before Story will be understood only by those responsive to the continuing influence of English case law after the Revolution. Again, Huber's prominence in England can be explained only by those familiar with Mansfield's Scottish connection; and with the Scottish law students' habit of studying law in the Dutch Republic. Huber's preeminence over other continental jurists in Scotland needs to be explained on the basis of where in their work he and others discussed conflict of laws, and the pattern of student book buying.

At this point the scholar will protest: to explain the development of American law in the nineteenth century, one surely cannot be expected to read Latin and French— luckily Huber's *Heedensdaegse Rechtsgeleertheyd* is translated—and, in other contexts, German. One surely cannot be expected to know Roman law and French law, the techniques of Dutch seventeenth-century jurists, and the state of Scottish legal education at that time. When the subject concerns the United States in general, one surely cannot be expected to appreciate the idiosyncrasies of the law of Louisiana.

Of course one cannot be expected to do these things. But one needs to do them, and many more, depending on the context, in order to do doctrinal American legal history. Accordingly, doctrinal legal history is not worth doing![1] It is not that scholars in legal history are lazy: it is only that foreign languages and foreign law are not part of their basic training and seem peripheral.

The standard approach to doctrinal legal history is smugly self-describing. An example that is very pertinent is in Lawrence M. Friedman, *History of American Law*:

> Story was not one to wear his erudition lightly. In his seminal work on the conflict of laws (1834), which systematized a new field (at least in the United States) out of virtually nothing, one page (360) has three lines of French and six of Latin, and quotes from Louis Boullenois, Achille Rodemburg, P. Voet,

J. Voet, C. D'Argentre, and U. Huberus, names that the American lawyer would find totally mysterious.

Story's erudition was not always so blatant; and this particular subject matter had hardly been treated by writers in English. Learning did not interfere with the main line of Story's argument, which proceeded clearly and stoutly, even gracefully at times.[2]

For Friedman, Story was too obviously and unnecessarily learned: his erudition was "blatant," but "[l]earning did not interfere with . . . Story's argument." The message is clear: we have no reason or need to follow Story in his erudition to understand the development of the law. Learning would be a barrier. Certainly, for Friedman, no purpose could be served for legal historians in reading people like Huber, "names that the American lawyer would find totally mysterious." Mysterious, therefore insignificant, and to be allowed to retain their mystery. But, as we have seen, not only was Huber frequently cited by judges, he was translated, and the translation was even republished. Friedman's own words should have given him pause: he writes that Story's *Conflict* "systematized a new field (at least in the United States) out of virtually nothing." But did it? Friedman, I believe, is claiming, not too accurately, that there was virtually no case law. So was Story creating conflicts law out of "virtually nothing"? Or were foreign doctrinal writings influential? Friedman has no intention of analyzing these questions, even though he says Story's "erudition was organic." He expresses his own view: Story's was "stultifying pedantry."[3]

But doctrinal legal history suffers from another handicap compared with other approaches. To use a fashionable expression, it is not sexy. It is titillating to believe that, when Grotius wrote, if only he ever had, it was not sexual intercourse but love that constituted a marriage, he was giving the legal version of the social phenomenon, observed in the seventeenth-century Netherlands, that married women were remarkably free in showing public affection to their husbands. It is boring to destroy the myth and show that Grotius said nothing of the kind, which in any event is a mistranslation of an ancient Roman and Byzantine text. The Dutch social phenomenon is not reflected in the law. It is seductive to believe that when William Blackstone was structuring his *Commentaries on the Law of England* he was setting forth his Weltanschauung, and the place of English law and himself in it. But how dreary it is to show that in large measure he was following the tabulation for the structure of Justinian's *Institutes* that had been drawn up by Dionysius Gothofredus (1549–1622).[4] It is exciting to think that in antebellum America judges chose to promote economic growth through the legal system, but it is unexciting to hold that actually they bumbled on with their judgments much as they had in other economic circumstances.[5]

If it were to be suggested that I have exaggerated what, from the perspective of doctrinal legal history, has to be known in order to plot the role of comity in early American law, and that it is enough to know that Huber was the accepted authority before Story, then I would respond that one would thereby forfeit the advantage of comparative law. It is precisely comparative law that can establish the relationship between law and society. Only an awareness of legal reasoning in seventeenth-century Europe would show how Huber's thesis was built up; only a knowledge of Scottish educational conditions would reveal that Huber was adopted in that country without being necessarily particularly suited to Scottish life; only the recognition that Mansfield was Scottish would indicate that Huber need not also have provided *the* approach for conflict of laws in England, and that the transplanting of Huber to the United States was not the result of careful weighing of possible alternatives.

Notes

Preface

1   I am awkwardly aware that my use of long quotations in this book is unfashionable. In part I plead that this is my preferred style; I wish to acquaint readers
directly with the sources. Alas, it is my sorry contention that many legal scholars either do not read or misreport the sources they purport to use. But, more
important, I have no choice. A major part of my argument is that texts have
been misunderstood. To demonstrate this I must quote *in extenso* the actual
passages by the persons misunderstood, and by the persons misunderstanding.
To show that the misunderstandings are not universal, necessary, or general, I
must quote the words of those who did understand or who may have understood the passages correctly. In large measure my argument rests on textual
analysis.

2   I use "State" with a capital when specifically considering a State of the United
States, but otherwise write "state."

3   Insofar as that section and art. IV, sec. 2, containing the "Privileges and Immunities" and "Fugitive Slaves" clauses, are denominated as the "Comity Clauses,"
the usage is later. "Comity" as used with regard to these clauses was not the
concern of Huber or Story as examined in this book.

4   A friend insists that, before Story, "choice of law" doctrines arose out of section 34 of the Judiciary Act of 1789, not out of Huber's theory. I totally reject
that view and mention it only to show that I am not unaware of the argument. Equally irrelevant to "choice of law" is *McElmoyle v. Cohen,* 13 Peters 312
(U.S., 1839).

5   Indeed, number 3 of 22 *Rutgers Law Journal* (1991), pp. 559ff., is a symposium
entitled "The Future of Personal Jurisdiction: a Symposium on *Burnham v.
Superior Court.*"

1   *Ulrich Huber and Comity*

1   This, of course, is not to deny that there are earlier well-reasoned cases. I would single out Chief Justice Isaac Parker's opinion in *Blanchard v. Russell,* 13 Mass. 1 (1816), which deals with both strands of conflicts law that are mentioned in the Introduction.

2   17 Martin 569, at p. 589. In this context the case is called "the climax of this prologue" by A. A. Ehrenzweig, *Private International Law: General Part* (Leyden, 1967), p. 52.

3   Bertrand D'Argentré (1519–1590) was a French judge and jurist.

4   Pp. 595ff.

5   "But Livermore, having lost his battle, went on with the war. Embittered by his defeat, he wrote his famous 'Dissertations,' the first American treatise on conflicts law" (Ehrenzweig, *Private International Law*, p. 53). The whole history of early conflict of laws in the United States is replete with curiosities, not the least of which is that the curious title of Livermore's book is cribbed from Louis Boullenois, *Dissertations sur les questions qui naissent de la contrariété des loix et des coutumes* (1732). The only earlier work on conflict of laws in English was Jabez Henry, *Treatise on the Difference Between Real and Personal Statutes* (1823). It seems to do nothing but repeat maxims of the civilian jurists: cf. D. J. Llewelyn Davies, "The Influence of Huber's *De Conflictu Legum* on English Private International Law," 18 *British Year Book of International Law* (1937), pp. 49ff., at p. 49.

6   Pp. 15f. For Livermore's discussion of comity see chap. 3 below.

7   This is not so much because issues of conflict of laws did not arise as because we have little information on Roman law in practice. The shaping force of Roman law as an intellectual system was the jurists, and they were remote from practice. They concentrated their attention on *iudicia legitima,* that is, trials between Roman citizens which took place in Rome or within the first milestone of the city, before a single judge.

8   See, e.g., E.-M. Meijers, "L'histoire des Principes fondamentaux du Droit international privé à partir du moyen âge," in *Recueil des Cours (Académie de Droit International)* 34, no. 3 (1934): 547ff.

9   Huber's §9 of his *Praelectiones juris romani et hodierni* 2.1.3 is exactly in point.

10 See, e.g., D. J. Llewelyn Davies, "Influence," p. 51; A. N. Sack, "Conflicts of Laws in the History of the English Law," in *Law, a Century of Progress, 1835–1935,* vol. 3 (New York, 1937), pp. 342ff. (the fullest and best single account); A. H. Charteris, "Scotland and the Common Law System of Private International Law," 11 *Australian Law Journal* (1938), pp. 378ff.; A. E. Anton, "The Introduction into English Practice of Continental Theories on the Conflict of Laws," 5 *International and Comparative Law Quarterly* (1956), pp. 534ff.; Dicey and Morris, *The Conflict of Laws,* vol. 1, 11th ed., ed. L. Collins (London, 1987), pp.

6f.; D. R. Coquillette, *The Civilian Writers of Doctors' Commons, London* (Berlin, 1988), pp. 34f., 97ff.

11 Cf. A. J. van der Aa, *Biographisch Woordenboek der Nederlanden*, vol. 3 (Haarlem, 1852), pp. 426ff.; T. J. Veen, *Recht en Nut, Studiën over en naar Aanleiding van Ulrik Huber (1636–1694)* (Zwolle, 1976), pp. 1ff.

12 His *Heedensdaegse Rechtsgeleertheyd*, written in contrast in Dutch, was worked upon when he was a judge: *Beginselen der Rechtkunde*, Tot den Leeser; *Rechtsgeleertheyd*, Voor-reeden.

13 "Nos ad detegendam hujus intricatissimae quaestionis subtilitatem, tria collocabimus axiomata, quae concessa, sicut omnino concedenda videntur, viam nobis ad reliqua planam redditura videntur."

14 Budé was a celebrated French humanist jurist (1467–1540).

15 On the *proemium* of the *Institutes*, §2. See also his *Positiones juris* 1.1.2 (1682). Comparisons of law as a science with mathematics or the use of mathematical terms were common. The best-known example is Leibnitz—see, e.g., M. H. Hoeflich, "Law and Geometry: Legal Science from Leibnitz to Langdell," 30 *American Journal of Legal History* (1986), pp. 95ff.—but closer to home for Huber is Grotius, *Inleiding tot de Hollandsche Rechtsgeleertheyd* (1631), 1.1.10–13. On axioms, see also G. C. J. J. van den Bergh, *The Life and Work of Gerard Noodt (1647–1725)* (Oxford, 1988), pp. 125f.

16 *Leges cujusque imperii vim habent intra terminus eiusdem Reipublicae omnesque ei subjectis obligant, nec ultra.*

17 *Pro subjectis imperio habendi sunt omnes, qui intra terminos ejusdem reperiuntur, sive in perpetuum, sive ad tempus ibi commorentur.*

18 *Rectores imperiorum id comiter agunt, ut jura cujusque populi intra terminos ejus exercita, teneant ubique suam vim, quatenus nihil potestati aut juri alterius imperantis ejusque civium praejudicetur.*

19 The notion that a rule of the *ius gentium* need not be expressed in a particular state to be valid law was a commonplace of the time: see, e.g., A. Vinnius, *In quattuor libros Institutionum Imperialium Commentarius* (1642), note to *naturalis ratio* in *J.* (Justinian's *Institutes*) 1.2.1.:

> The *jus gentium* is not to be judged from the institutions of peoples, but from what natural reason pronounces to be just, that is the knowledge inherent in the minds of men of the honest and base, just and unjust; for example, incests, adulteries, thefts are base and illicit by nature; even if nations were found among whom these were permitted or not punished.
>
> [Jus gentium non ex institutis populorum aestimandum est, sed ex eo, quod justum esse ipsa naturalis dictat ratio, id est, insita animis hominum notitia honesti et turpis, justi et injusti V.G. Incesta, adulteria, furta natura turpia et illicita sunt; etiamsi gentes repertae, in quibus haec permissa aut non punita.]

20 Huber, *Heedensdaegse Rechtsgeleertheyd* 1.2.47.

21 See P. Stein, "Bartolus, The Conflict of Laws and the Roman Law," in *Multum non*

Multa: Festschrift für Kurt Lipstein, ed. P. Feuerstein and C. Parry (Heidelberg, 1980), pp. 251ff.

22 On Justinian's *Code* 1.4, *De summa trinitati*, gloss *Quod si Bononiensis*, §19. "Ex praedictis possunt solvi multae quaestiones. Statutum est Assisii, ubi est celebratus contractus dotis et matrimonii, quod vir lucretur etiam (qu. tertiam?) partem dotis, uxore moriente sine liberis: in hac vero civitate Perusii, unde est vir, statutum est quod vir lucretur dimidiam; quid spectabitur? Certe statutum terrae viri: ut *d. 1. exigere*."

23 "Exigere dotem mulier debet illic, ubi maritus domicilium habuit, non ubi instrumentum dotale conscriptum est: nec enim id genus contractus est, ut et eum locum spectari oporteat, in quo instrumentum dotis factum est, quam eum, in cuius domicilium et ipsa mulier per condicionem matrimonii erat reditura."

24 See the discussion by A. Watson, *The Making of the Civil Law* (Cambridge, Mass., 1981), pp. 53ff., on N. Everardus, *Loci argumentorum legales* (1516).

25 "Ex quo liquet, hanc rem non ex simplici jure Civili, sed ex commodis et tacito populorum consensu esse petendam: quia sicut leges alterius populi apud alium directe valere non possunt, ita commerciis et usu gentium promiscuo nihil foret magis incommodum, quam si res jure certi loci validae, mox alibi diversitate Juris infirmarentur, quae est ratio tertii axiomatis: quod, uti nec prius, nullum videtur habere dubium."

26 "Inter ea, quae diversi populi sibi in vicem debent, merito refertur, observantia Legum aliarum Civitatum in aliis Imperiis; ad quam etsi non teneantur ex pacto vel necessitate subordinationis; tamen promiscui usus ratio inter gentes mutuam hac in parte flagitat indulgentiam."

27 See the texts quoted by Meijers, "Histoire," p. 664 n. 1.

28 "Histoire," p. 667.

29 "Inde fluit haec Positio: *Cuncta negotia et acta tam in judicio quam extra judicium, seu mortis causa sive inter vivos, secundum jus certi loci rite celebrata valent, etiam ubi diversa juris observatio viget, ac ubi sic inita, quemadmodum facta sunt, non valerent.* E contra, negotia et acta certo loco contra leges ejus loci celebrata, cum sint ab initio invalida, nusquam valere possunt."

30 "Sub hac tamen exceptione; si rectores alterius populi exinde notabili incommodo afficerentur, ut hi talibus actis atque negotiis usum effectumque dare non teneantur, secundum tertii axiomatis limitationem. Digna res est, quae exemplis declaretur."

31 "Fiction" is not used here in the technical sense of a clause called *fictio* inserted into Roman pleadings.

32 One might add *Digest* 42.5.3 (on a judicial sale): "Or where he made the contract. But it is deemed to be contracted not where it was entered into, but where payment is due." *Digest* 44.7.21 was relied upon in court—for instance, in the 1792 Scottish case of *Armour v. Campbell,* M. 4476.

33 Sec. 8.

34 Sec. 5; quoted below, chap. 4.

35 "Titius in Frisiae finibus homine percusso in capite, qui sequenti nocte, sanguine multo e naribus emisso, at bene potus atque cenatus, erat exstinctus; Titius, inquam, evasit in Transisulaniam. Ibi captus, ut videtur volens, mox judicatus et absolutus est, tanquam homine non ex vulnere exstincto. Haec sententia mittitur in Frisiam et petitur impunitas rei absoluti. Quamquam ratio absolutionis non erat a fide veri aliena, tamen Curia Frisiae vim sententiae veniamque reo polliceri, Transisulanis licet postulantibus, gravata est. Quia tali in viciniam effugio et processu adfectato, jurisdictioni Frisiorum eludendae via nimis parata futura videbatur, quae est tertii axiomatis exceptionis ratio."

36 The common-law rule in the United States is that there is no murder if the victim survives for a year and a day. For the analogous rule in biblical law, see Exodus 21.18.

37 *De statutis* 11.1.6.

38 Huber does not frame it that way, but that is how it works out with his examples.

39 "Matrimonium pertinet etiam ad has regulas. Si licitum est eo loco, ubi contractum et celebratum est, ubique validum erit effectumque habebit, sub eadem exceptione, praejudicii aliis non creandi; cui licet addere, si exempli nimis sit abominandi; ut si incestum juris gentium in secundo gradu contingeret alicubi esse permissum; quod vix est ut usu venire possit."

40 It was accepted doctrine that it might be possible to find a people that did not accept a proposition of the *ius gentium,* and that the proposition would nonetheless remain *ius gentium:* see, e.g., the passage from Vinnius in J.1.2.1, quoted above in n. 20; cf. D. Cavallarius (1724–1781), *Institutiones iuris romani* 1.2.1.3.

41 "18. Wat van Testamenten in dese exempelen is gezegt, heeft buiten zwijvel ook plaets in handelingen onder levende, gelijk zijn, allerhande Contracten, die aengegaen zijnde nae de rechten ende costumen van yder plaets, over al moeten gelden, soo wel in, als buiten recht, olk self in sulke plaetsen dar se anders verboden zijn.

"19. By exempel; Op eenige plaetsen mag verboden zijn, gelijk alhier voor deesen is verboden geweest, om brandewijn of eenige andere waeren te verkopen; indien echter een Burger van het Landt wort aangesprooken om brandewijn gekocht ter plaetse, daer se vrijlijk mochte gekocht worden, soo moet hy gecondemneert worden, ook immers in die plaetsen, daer't verboden is sulke waeren te kopen ende te verkopen, om dat het Contract goedt zijnde dar het gemaekt is, overal wordt erkent, om te gelden tusschen Partijen.

"20. Maer als Partijen hadden een koop geflooten van brandewijn te leveren in t'Landt, daer sy verboden is, daer uit soude geen actie vallen in dat Landt, om dat het soude strijden met het recht ende macht van dat selve Landtschap, 't welk binnen haere palen die leeveringe heeft verboden.

"21. Stelt nu eens wederom; Een uytlander heeft aen een Fries alhier verkocht ende geleevert in de Provintie, brandewijn ofte andere verboden waeren; by kan uit sulken koop nae reeden van Rechte nergens actie maken, self niet buiten de Provintie, indien by den koper vont; immens niet uit kracht van de koop, om dat sy beide gedaen habben wat hut verboden was te doen; ten waer de billijkheyt om by sondere omstandigheden eenig remedie extraordinaris tegen den baetsoekenden koper mochte verschaffen.

"22. Een ander; in een Stadt is verboden brandewijn te drinken, de lieden gaen even buiten de Jurisdictie van de Stadt, en doen't aldaer. Alhoewel de handelinge daer te plaetse geoorlost is, soo geest sy evenwel geen aenspraek in die Stadt, om dat het is tot merkelijk ongerijf ende wanordere desselfs; maer elders valt 'er aenspraek van.

"23. Wederom, 't is verboden even buiten de Jurisdictie der Stadt te gaen drinken, om des Stadts excijsen niet te verminderen, gelijk daer van exempelen zijn; de Burgers doen't evenwel; sy zijn tot harent straf-baer over't seit; maer de handel is geoorlost, en daerom geest sy overal aenspraek, behalven in die Stadt, om reeden ten voorigen artikele verhaelt."

I have followed the excellent translation by P. Gane, *Huber's Jurisprudence of My Time* (Durban, 1939), p. 13.

42   "Statutum loci extra territorium, e comitate et aequitate saepe servatur."
43   "Denique nonnunquam, dum populus vicinus vicini mores comiter vult observare, et ne multa bene gesta turbarentur, de moribus, statuta territorium statuentis, inspecto effectu, solent egredi."
44   4.3.15,17; 10.1.14; 11.1.5,6; see also *De natura bonorum mobilium et immobilium* 23.4,14.
45   "Malim tamen, id ita obtinere, non tam de jure, quam quidem de humanitate, dum populus vicini decreta populi comiter observat, ut multorum evitetur confusio." *De statutis*, 4.3.15.
46   Voet, *De statutis* 11. 16. 17; *Commentarius ad Pandectas* 5.1.67; 42.1.41; 48.3.1; Sande, *Definitiones* 1.1.6; Groenewegen, *De legibus abrogatis* (1669) in *C.* (=Justinian's *Code*) 3.15.1.
47   See, above all, Meijers, "Histoire," pp. 664ff.
48   "Influence," p. 58.
49   This whole subject is, as I have said, replete with curiosities. Another is that Llewelyn Davies himself believed that the term "comity" as used by the Dutch jurists was misunderstood, as meaning that the recognition of foreign law depended on the mere courtesy of the state granting such recognition. He then rightly observed that Huber associated *comitas gentium* with *ius gentium,* and that the rules of conflict of laws rested on general interest and tacit consent of all states. And he concluded that this doctrine was understood and accepted by Story ("Influence," pp. 57f.).
50   Huber, *Praelectiones*, 2.1.3.7.
51   For England, *De la Vega v. Vianna,* 1 B. & Ad. 284 (1830); *British Linen Co. v. Drummond,* 10 B. & C. 903 (1830); *Don v. Lippmann,* 5 Cl. & F. 1 (1837); *Ler-*

oux v. Brown, 12 C.B. 801 (1852). For the United States, *Lodge v. Phelps*, 1 Johns. Cas. 139 (New York, 1799); *Pearsall v. Dwight*, 2 Mass. R. 83 (1806); *Andrews v. Herriot*, 4 Cowen 508 (New York, 1825).

52   3 Johns. Ch. 190 (1817), at p. 202.
53   On Justinian's *Code* 1.4, *De summa trinitati*, gloss *Quod si Bononiensis*, §15; *Digest* 22.5.3.
54   Sec. 14.
55   This rule was already accepted (if without Huber's reasoning) in various countries: see, for example, the 1623 Scottish case of *Henderson's Children v. Murray*, M. 4481 (where Bartolus and the Gloss are cited).
56   Sec. 15.
57   Secs. 12, 13.

2 *Joseph Story and Comity*

1   For Story's knowledge and use of Roman and civil law see M. H. Hoeflich, "John Austin and Joseph Story: Two Nineteenth Century Perspectives on the Utility of the Civil Law for the Common Lawyer," 29 *American Journal of Legal History* (1985), pp. 36ff., at pp. 56ff.
2   P. 19.
3   P. 30.
4   See, e.g., *Commentaries on the Conflict of Laws* (hereinafter cited as *Conflict*, pp. 31ff.
5   *Conflict*, p. 32. Actually, there is no sign in Huber that he is following the practice of nations. Huber does cite Grotius, *De iure belli ac pacis* (On the law of war and peace), 2.11.5, but not for anything relevant to Story's proposition.
6   *Conflict*, p. 32.
7   See e.g., T. R. R. Cobb, *An Inquiry into the Law of Negro Slavery in the United States of America* (Philadelphia, 1858), p. 144; A. K. Kuhn, "Private International Law," 12 *Columbia Law Review* (1912), pp. 44ff., at p. 47; E. G. Lorenzen, "Story's Commentaries on the Conflict of Laws—One Hundred Years After," 48 *Harvard Law Review* (1934), pp. 15ff., at pp. 17, 35f.; J. K. Beach, "Uniform Interstate Enforcement of Vested Rights," 27 *Yale Law Journal* (1918), pp. 656ff., at p. 657; H. E. Yntema, "The Historic Bases of Private International Law," 2 *American Journal of Comparative Law* (1956), pp. 297ff., at p. 307; K. H. Nadelmann, "Joseph Story's Contribution to American Conflicts Law," 5 *American Journal of Legal History* (1961), pp. 230ff.; A. E. Anton, *Private International Law* (Edinburgh, 1967), pp. 22f.; G. C. Hazard, "A General Theory of State-Court Jurisdiction," *Supreme Court Review* (1965), pp. 241ff., at pp. 259ff. (also with qualifications that do not concern us here and that are not entirely convincing, since Hazard is insufficiently attentive to Huber); W. R. Leslie, "The Influence of Joseph Story's Theory of Conflict of Laws on Constitutional Nationalism," 35

Mississippi Valley Historical Review (1948), pp. 204ff. (noting a qualification of
Story to Huber at p. 210); A. A. Ehrenzweig, *Private International Law: General
Part* (Leyden, 1967), p. 54 (designating Huber as Story's "idol"); R. M. Cover,
Justice Accused (New Haven, 1975), p. 84; Paul Finkelman, *An Imperfect Union:
Slavery, Federalism, and Comity* (Chapel Hill, 1981), p. 13; J. N. Drobak, "The
Federalism Theme in Personal Jurisdiction," 68 *Iowa Law Review* (1983), pp.
1015ff., at p. 1027 and n. 60; W. J. Hosten, A. B. Edwards, C. Nathan, F. Bosman,
Introduction to South African Law and Legal Theory (Durban, 1977), pp. 830f.;
V. C. Hopkins, *Dred Scott's Case* (New York, 1951), pp. 150f. (with a qualification); D. C. K. Chow, "Limiting *Erie* in a New Age of International Law: Toward
a Federal Common Law of International Choice of Law," 74 *Iowa Law Review*
(1988), pp. 165ff. at pp. 170ff.; *Burnham v. Superior Court*, Marin County, 110
S. Ct. (1990), at p. 2122 n. 8 (with qualifications).
8 *Conflict*, pp. 33f.
9 See, e.g., *Traité des obligations*, preliminary article, §1. For a slightly different
version of this notion of perfect and imperfect obligations, see, E. de Vattel, *Le
droit des gens* (1708), préliminaires, §17.
10 *Conflict*, pp. 35f.
11 *Imperfect Union*, p. 21.
12 Here Story cites Huber. He also refers to the second edition of James Kent,
Commentaries on American Law 2 (New York, 1832), 457, and this is discussed
in chap. 3; to *Greenwood v. Curtis*, 6 Mass. 358 R. (1810), which is also discussed in that chapter; and to two other cases, which contain only very general
statements made *obiter: Trasher v. Everhart*, 3 G. & J. 234 (Md., 1831) and
Pearsall v. Dwight, 2 Mass. R. 83 (1806).
13 *Commentary*, p. 203f.
14 Pp. 470ff.
15 Of course, an important point for Best is that the English legislature had abolished the trade in slaves, thus showing their disapprobation of slavery, p. 470.
16 Huber's rule does have a very different basis: his axioms are based on *ius gentium*
as being part of Roman law.

3 *Explanation*

1 P. 364; see appendix B below.
2 P. 455.
3 P. 457.
4 17 Martin 569 (La.).
5 Pp. 571f.
6 Pp. 585f.
7 Pp. 26f.
8 Pp. 12f. He treats Huber more fully, but with no more respect, on a different
matter, pp. 42ff.

9 Such was the attention paid to *Saul v. His Creditors* that it is the sole case cited by W. Guthrie in the preface (written in 1849) to his translation of Savigny: *A Treatise on the Conflict of Laws by F. K. von Savigny* (Edinburgh, 1869).

10 W. W. Story, *Life and Letters of Joseph Story*, vol. 2 (Boston, 1851), p. 110.

11 *Conflict*, p. 36 and n. 1.

12 The seven cases: *Lodge v. Phelps*, 1 Johns. Cas. 139 (N.Y., 1799); *Van Reimsdyk v. Kane*, 1 Gallison 371 (Circuit Court, D. R.I., 1813); *Blanchard v. Russell*, 13 Mass. R. 1 (1816); *Prentiss v. Savage*, 13 Mass. R. 20 (1816); *Harvey v. Richards*, 1 Mason 381 (Circuit Court, D. Mass., 1818); *LeRoy v. Crowninshield*, 2 Mason 151 (Circuit Court, D. Mass., 1820); *Brown v. Richardson*, 13 Martin 202 (La., 1823).

13 In medieval English law where there was nonfeasance on an agreement, and the nonfeasance consisted of a failure to pay money, the only remedy normally available was the writ of debt. Debt was an unsatisfactory remedy, and there were attempts to increase the scope of *assumpsit*. One of these was *insimul computassent*. When merchants dealt together, *assumpsit* could be brought on the consideration that "they had accounted together," and the debt was due: see, e.g., A. W. B. Simpson, *A History of the Common Law of Contract* (Oxford, 1975), pp. 281ff.; J. H. Baker, *Introduction to English Legal History*, 2d ed. (London, 1979), pp. 339ff.; S. F. C. Milsom, *Historical Foundations of the Common Law*, 2d ed. (Toronto, 1981), pp. 339ff.; J. H. Baker and S. F. C. Milsom, *Sources of English Legal History* (London, 1986), pp. 406ff.

14 *Greenwood v. Curtis* at p. 377.

15 P. 378f.

16 P. 380.

17 See A. Watson, "Some Notes on Mackenzie's *Institutions* and the European Legal Tradition," *Ius Commune* (1989), pp. 303ff. For Huber himself, see his *Praelectiones*, 1.2, §4 on the *Institutes*.

18 Pp. 380f.

19 P. 381.

20 But Judge Theodore Sedgwick, who had left the bench before the opinion was pronounced, instructed the reporter to insert a note of his dissent. He did argue that if the consideration of a promise was immoral or if the promise was immoral no action lay, and the parts of a translation should not be split. He contended vehemently that the present contract was immoral and unenforceable in Massachusetts: note on the case beginning at p. 362.

21 But it should be noted that also in 1822 Story was rather imprecise about comity: see *United States v. The La Jeune Eugénie* at p. 840 in the report in 26 *Federal Cases* (no. 15551). But he was not confronting the issue directly.

22 *Conflict*, p. 10 n. 1; p. 36 and n. 1.

23 *Conflict*, pp. 14 n. 1; 29; 29 n. 2; 33; 33 n. 2.

24 *Conflict*, pp. 4 n. 1; 7 n. 2; 10 n. 2; 13 n. 6; 15 n. 2; 16 nn. 1, 2; 18 n. 2; 23; 33 n. 1; 34 n. 1.

25   *Supreme Court Justice Joseph Story: Statesman of the Old Republic* (Chapel Hill, 1985), pp. 296ff.

26   *Story*, p. 297.

27   Newmyer's view, it should be noted, would not be relevant to an acceptance of a Huber or non-Huber theory of comity.

28   There was an exception for the domestic slaves of congressmen from other states, foreign ministers, and consuls. For cases involving the statute see, e.g., *Butler v. Hopper*, 1 Wash. C.C. 499 (Federal Case No. 2,241) (1806); *Ex parte Simmons*, 4 Wash. C.C. 396 (Federal Case No. 12,863) (1823). The ringing section 1 of the Declaration of Rights of Vermont in 1777 does not address the issue.

29   *Winny v. Whitesides*, 1 Mo. 472 (1824), in which Huber in Dallas's translation is cited; *Merry v. Tiffin and Menard*, 1 Mo. 725 (1827); *Milly (a woman of color) v. Smith*, 2 Mo. 36 (1828); *Vincent (a man of color) v. Duncan*, 2 Mo. 214 (1830); *Ralph (a man of color) v. Duncan*, 3 Mo. 194 (1833); *Julia (a woman of color) v. McKinney*, 3 Mo. 270 (1833); *Nat (a man of color) v. Ruddle*, 3 Mo. 400 (1834); cf. *La Grange v. Chouteau*, 2 Mo. 19 (1828). From 1836, just after the publication of Story's *Conflict*, comes the leading Missouri precedent to the same effect: *Rachael (a woman of color) v. Walker*, 4 Mo. 350; see also *Wilson (a colored man) v. Melvin*, 4 Mo. 592 (1837). The Northwest Ordinance of 1787 was also a relevant factor in the decisions. For an early, very sophisticated, case recognizing the importance of foreign jurisdictions, but accepting the priority of an overriding statute, see *Mahoney v. Ashton*, 4 Harris and McHenry 295 (Md. 1799).

30   *Conflict*, p. 106.

31   *Conflict*, pp. 106f. In support of Story's proposition here one might cite the first quotation in this chapter from Parsons in *Greenwood v. Curtis*.

32   Grotius, *Inleiding tot de Hollandsche Rechtsgeleertheyd* 1.5.11. For a few of the pamphlets written with passion in England at the time, see the references in A. Watson, *Society and Legal Change* (Edinburgh, 1977), p. 138 n. 17. For a recent account see S. Wolfram, *In-Laws and Outlaws, Kinship and Marriage in England* (New York, 1987), pp. 30ff.

33   *Conflict*, pp. 92f.

34   The case is discussed in chap. 5.

35   17 Martin 569 (La., 1827).

36   9 *American Jurist* (1833), pp. 490ff.

37   1 Wash. C.C. 499 (Federal Case No. 2,241) (1806), and 4 Wash. C.C. 396 (Federal Case No. 12,863) (1823), respectively.

38   See, e.g., Simon à Groenewegen, *De legibus abrogatis* on J.1.8, and the authorities he cites. At some point, which I have not been able to document before 1736, an exception was introduced where the slave in question was enslaved in a Dutch colony (C. van Bynkershoek, *Observationes Tumultuariae*, no. 2966).

On the case see also T. R. R. Cobb, *An Inquiry Into the Law of Negro Slavery in the United States* (Philadelphia, 1858), p. 143 n. 1, and the authors he cites: also Alan Watson, *Slave Law in the Americas* (Athens, Ga., 1989), pp. 104f.

39   The cases are discussed in the sixth edition at pp. 127ff.

40   16 Peters 539 (U.S., 1842).

41   P. 622.

42   P. 612.

43   P. 612. See also Story's *Commentaries on the Constitution of the United States* (1833), p. 676.

44   See the sources cited by J. McClellan, *Joseph Story and the American Constitution* (Norman, 1971), pp. 297ff.; R. Cover, *Justice Accused* (New Haven, 1975), pp. 238ff.

45   2 Mason 409 (Federal Case No. 15551; in 26 *Federal Cases*, 832 at p. 845) (C.C.D. Mass., 1822).

46   It has been suggested to me that one might argue from the structure of chapter 2 of Story's *Conflict* that he was deliberately misstating Huber's comity. Story brings in Huber at the end of the chapter, the argument goes, to give the appearance that Huber was a support for Story's doctrine. Story had Huber in mind all along and knew he would have to contend with axiom 3. Huber meant axiom 3 to flow from the first two, but Story disjoined axiom 3 from the other two to turn Huber around. Story wrote: "From these two maxims or propositions, there flows a third, and that is, that whatever force and obligation the laws of one country have in another, depends solely upon the laws, and municipal regulations of the latter, that is to say, upon its own proper jurisprudence and polity, and upon its own express or tacit consent" (*Conflict*, p. 24). Story has restated Huber's exception as though it were the rule.

I agree that Story had Huber in mind all along, and deliberately left his discussion of him until late in the chapter so that his own propositions seem to have their own validity but to be bolstered by Huber. But this is in no way inconsistent with Story accidentally misunderstanding Huber. Also, Huber does not intend axiom 3 to flow from axioms 1 and 2.

I stress the difficulties for believing that Story deliberately misrepresented Huber, because I am aware there will be a reluctance to accept that a doctrine so important in American life as Story's comity could have resulted from a mistake. Indeed, a friend who produced no evidence for deliberate manipulation by Story was so incensed by the proposition that a significant legal change could result from an accident that she called me "wrong-headed." The belief that law reflects societal conditions dies hard.

47   See app. B.

48   Sec. 2.

49   Secs. 2, 3, 9, 11.

4   Pre-Story

1   Conflict of laws loomed large in U.S. slave law: see, e.g., T. R. R. Cobb, *An Inquiry Into the Law of Negro Slavery* (Philadelphia, 1858).

2   (Chapel Hill, 1981), p. 21.

3   The other so-called "comity" provisions of the U.S. Constitution are not germane to the issues in this book. But for the meaning of art. IV., sec. 1, the "Full Faith and Credit" clause; art. IV., sec. 2, cl. 1, "Interstate Privileges and Immunities"; art. IV., sec. 2, cl. 2, "Fugitives from Justice," see, e.g., E. Dumbauld, *The Constitution of the United States* (Norman, Okla., 1964), pp. 386ff. An important U.S. Supreme Court case involving Story, which depended solely on the "Full Faith and Credit" clause and the subsequent federal act of 26 May 1790, chap. 11, is *Mills v. Duryee,* 7 Cranch 481 (U.S., 1813). See also, post-Story, *McElmoyle v. Cohen,* 13 Peters 312 (U.S., 1839).

4   The mistake is revealing in quite a different way. Such was the success of Story's theory that here and throughout Finkelman writes as if there were no other view.

5   For the history of this clause see, e.g., Dumbauld, *Constitution,* pp. 420f.

6   See, e.g., C. Collier and J. L. Collier, *Decision in Philadelphia: The Constitutional Convention of 1787* (New York, 1986), pp. 175ff.; W. M. Wiecek, *The Sources of Antislavery Constitutionalism in America, 1760–1848* (Ithaca, 1977), pp. 78ff.; P. S. Paludan, "Hercules Unbound: Lincoln, Slavery, and the Intention of the Framers," to appear in *The Constitution, Law, and American Life: Critical Aspects of the Nineteenth Century Experience,* ed. D. G. Nieman.

7   The term "comity of nations" is later. The *Oxford English Dictionary* attributes its introduction to Story in 1834. But it is earlier. It goes back at least to 1810; *Green v. Sarmiento,* Peters. C.C. 74; Wash. C.C. 17 (Federal Case No. 5760).

8   Finkelman adopts a different position in *Imperfect Union,* pp. 34ff., esp. at p. 40. For him it is unlikely that the southerners saw the free transit of masters with their slaves as a remote problem, and he suggests the southerners may have thought it impossible to win more concessions for slavery. But this would not explain their complete silence on the matter. As far as I am aware they did not even discuss the matter among themselves: see, for instance, the absence of any mention in R. M. Weir, "South Carolina: Slavery and the Structure of the Union," in M. A. Gillespie and M. Lienesch, eds., *Ratifying the Constitution* (Lawrence, Kans., 1989), pp. 201ff. Cobb argues that the "Full Faith and Credit" clause of the U.S. Constitution imposed a strict obligation of comity between the States (*Inquiry,* pp. 186ff.).

9   See chap. 5, n. 3. Indeed, by 1787 no American reports had been published; see E. C. Surrency, "Law Reports in the United States," 25 *American Journal of Legal History* (1981), pp. 48ff.

10   At the period in question there was developing a system of "American law"

based on the cases, though naturally it was accepted that there were differences in law between the States. At that time there was no even moderately strict ranking of precedents in the United States on the basis of their source from another State. This emerges clearly from James Kent's discussion of precedent (*Commentaries on American Law*, vol. 1, 1st ed. [New York, 1826], pp. 439ff.). Of course, individual judges, such as Mansfield, might be given superior weight. On the subject of conflict of laws in the United States there are frequent references to Scottish and English cases, and I have found no hostility, in this field, to the use of English law. Accordingly, I will use English and American case law equally, though I will make plain the provenance of a case. English cases after 1775 should have no authority in the United States, but writers such as Kent and Story make no distinction in the use of pre-1775 and post-1775 judgments. On the meaning of American law as opposed to English law in section 34 of the Judiciary Act of 1789, see W. J. Ritz and others, *Rewriting the History of the Judiciary Act of 1789* (Norman, Okla., 1990), pp. 262ff., esp. at p. 148, pp. 149ff.

11 2 Salk. 665.

12 But see Lord Mansfield's discussion of fictions in *Mostyn v. Fabrigas,* 1 Cowp. R. 161 (1774), at pp. 177f. *Scrimshire v. Scrimshire,* 2 Hag. Corr. 395 (1752) seems to be unique among conflicts cases for its continental learning at an early date. Justinian's *Digest* and *Code*, Gaill, Donellus, Sanchez, Mynsinger, and J. Voet are all cited. My point here is not that English attorneys, especially those in Doctors' Commons, might not be learned in continental thinking, but that the state of the law prevented any such learning from appearing in what would now be treated as conflicts cases. For civilian learning in Doctors' Commons and for jurisdiction in the law maritime see D. R. Coquillette, *The Civilian Writers of Doctors' Commons, London* (Berlin, 1988), pp. 44ff., 97ff., 149ff.

13 1 Cowp. 341. For the early history see Cheshire and North's *Private International Law*, 11th ed., ed. P. M. North and J. J. Fawcett (London, 1987), pp. 23ff.

14 3 Mer. 67.

15 P. 79.

16 1 Bl. W. 234 at p. 257; 2 Burr. 1077.

17 M. 4533 (1713).

18 See A. E. Anton, "The Introduction into English Practice of Continental Theories on the Conflict of Law," 5 *International and Comparative Law Quarterly* (1956), pp. 534ff., at pp. 538f.

19 *Emory v. Greenough,* 3 Dallas 369 (U.S., 1797).

20 Pp. 449ff.

21 *Robinson v. Bland,* 1 Bl. W. 234 at p. 257; 2 Burr. 1077.

22 1 Cowp. R. 341.

23 "Quo de testamentis habuimus, locum etiam habet in actibus inter vivos; proinde contractus celebrati secundum jus loci, in quo contrahuntur, ubique tam in Jure quam extra judicium, etiam ubi hoc modo celebrati non vale-

rent, sustinentur; idque non tantum de forma, sed etiam de materia contractus affirmandum est. Ex. gr. In certo loco merces quaedam prohibitae sunt; si vendantur ibi, contractus est nullus: verum si merx eadem alibi sit vendita, ubi non erat interdicta, et ex eo contractu agatur in locis ubi interdictum viget, Emptor condemnabitur; quia contractus inde ab initio validus fuit. Verum si merces venditae, in altero loco, ubi prohibitae sunt, essent tradendae, jam non fieret condemnatio; quia repugnaret hoc juri et commodo Reip. quae merces prohibuit, secundum limitationem axiomatis tertii. Ex adverso, si clam fuerint venditae merces, in loco ubi prohibitae sunt, emptio venditio non valet ab initio nec parit actionem quounque loco instituatur, utique ad traditionem urgendam: nam si traditione facta, precium solvere nollet emptor, non tam è contractu quam re obligaretur, quatenus cum alterius damno locupletior fieri vellet."

24 Sec. 3.
25 See C. P. Rodgers, "Continental Literature and the Development of the Common Law by the King's Bench, c. 1750–1800," in *Comparative Studies in Continental and Anglo-American Legal History*, vol. 2: *Courts and the Development of Common Law*, ed. V. Piergiovanni (Berlin, 1987), pp. 161ff., at pp. 182ff.
26 But Story approved of the reasoning in this case and he cites Huber in connection with it (*Conflict*, pp. 208f.).
27 1 Binn. 336.
28 The reference is to *The Ship Columbus*, which is discussed in app. C.
29 P. 342.
30 Presumably the reference to Marriott is in the passage quoted later in this chapter, which also concerns *The Ship Columbus*; the reference to Mansfield is in p. 348.
31 6 Brown 577, at p. 596.
32 4 Cowen 508 (New York).
33 P. 510.
34 *Decouche v. Savetier,* 3 Johns. Ch. 190, at p. 202. See also the later English case of *Birtwhistle v. Vardell,* 7 CP & F. 895 (1839–40), at p. 915, per Lord Brougham.
35 1 Rand. 15.
36 P. 19.
37 Pp. 23f.
38 *Holmes v. Remsen,* 4 Johns. Ch. 460 (1820), at pp. 469f.
39 At p. 470.
40 See, e.g., *Bruce v. Bruce,* 6 Brown 566 (England/Scotland, 1790), at p. 573; *Lodge v. Phelps,* 1 Johns. Cas. 139 (New York, 1799); *Pearsall v. Dwight,* 2 Mass. R. 83 (1806), at p. 89; *Doe v. Vardill,* 5 B. & C. 439 (England, 1826); *West Cambridge v. Lexington,* 1 Pick. 506 (Mass., 1827); *De la Vega v. Vianna,* 1 B. & Ad. 284 (England, 1830), at p. 287; *British Linen Co. v. Drummond,* 10 B. & C. 903 (Scot-

land, 1830). In *Balfour v. Scott,* 6 Brown 550 (Scotland, 1793) Johannes Voet
was praised and followed, and Huber is not mentioned: Voet, but not Huber,
was used in argument in *Tovey v. Lindsay,* 1 Dow 124 (Scotland/England, 1813).

41 *An Anniversary Discourse Delivered before the New York Historical Society, Decem-*
ber 2, 1818, p. 65. The case referred to is *The Ship Columbus,* which is discussed
in app. C.

42 Cf., e.g., S. Jay, "Origins of Federal Common Law: Part Two," 133 *University of*
Pennsylvania Law Review (1985), pp. 1231ff., at p. 1284. See also *Société Natio-*
nale Industrielle Aérospatiale v. U.S. District Court, 482 U.S. 522 (1986), *per*
Justice Stevens, p. 543 n. 27.

43 K. H. Nadelmann, "Joseph Story's Contribution to American Conflicts Law: A
Comment," 5 *American Journal of Legal History* (1961), pp. 230ff., at 231.

44 7 Serg. & Rawle 378.

45 Pp. 383, 385.

46 P. 383.

47 Gil. 143.

48 For some other pre-Story cases involving a recognition of comity between free
and slave states see *Porter v. Butler,* 3 H. & McH. 168 (Md., 1785); *Selectmen of*
Windsor v. Jacob, 2 Tyler 192 (Ver., 1802); *Rankin v. Lydia,* 2 A. K. Marshall 813
(Ken., 1820); *Davis v. Jacquin,* 5 H. & J. 100 (Md., 1820); *Winny v. Whitesides,*
1 Mo. 472 (1824) (Huber cited with approval); *Lunsford v. Coquillon,* 2 Mart.
(N.S.) 401 (Louisiana, 1824) (Huber cited with approval); *Milly (a woman of*
color) v. Smith, 2 Mo. 36 (1828); *Hunter v. Fulcher,* 1 Leigh 172 (Va., 1829); *Julia*
(a woman of color) v. McKinney, 3 Mo. 270 (1833); *Ralph (a man of color) v.*
Ruddle, 3 Mo. 400 (1834). See also *Pearsall v. Dwight,* 2 Mass. R. 83 (1806);
Van Reimsdyk v. Kane, 1 Gallison 371 (Federal Case No. 16872) (Circuit Court,
D. R.I., 1813).

5 Post-Story

1 See also the anonymous author of the note introducing the reprint of Dallas's
translation of Huber in 1 *Carolina Law Journal* (1831), pp. 449ff.

2 See W. W. Story, *Life and Letters of Joseph Story,* vol. 2 (Boston, 1851), p. 166;
see also Story, *Conflicts,* p. 9.

3 It is this fact that brings out the full significance of Dallas's translation of Huber:
Emory v. Greenough, 3 Dallas 369 (U.S., 1797).

4 See, e.g., W. W. Story, *Life* 2:142.

5 E. G. Lorenzen, "Story's Commentaries on the Conflict of Laws—One Hundred
Years After," 48 *Harvard Law Review* (1934), pp. 15ff., at p. 18; accepted by
D. J. Llewelyn Davies, "The Influence of Huber's *De Conflictu Legum* on English
Private International Law," 18 *British Yearbook of International Law* (1937), pp.

49ff. at p. 50; R. Kent Newmyer, *Supreme Court Justice Joseph Story* (Chapel Hill, 1985), p. 296.

6   See Newmyer, *Story*, p. 296.

7   *Comparative Commentaries on Private International Law or Conflicts of Laws* (New York, 1937), p. 20.

8   On criticism, see Newmyer, *Story*, p. 299 and the authors he cites; most recently, associate justices Antonin Scalia and Byron R. White in *Burnham v. Superior Court*, Marin County, 110 S. Ct. 2105 (1990). On praise, see, e.g., Newmyer, *Story*, pp. 298f.; and the letters recorded in W. W. Story, *Life*, 2:167ff.

9   As early as the following year the English chief justice, Sir Nicholas Tindal, declared it "a work which it would be unjust to mention without at the same time paying a tribute to the learning, acuteness, and accuracy of its author": *Huber v. Steiner*, 2 Bing 202 [N.C.], at p. 211. See also Lord Brougham in *Don v. Lippmann* [1837] 3 Cl. & F. 1, at p. 16. A fine example in the United States, from Chief Justice Taney, of *Dred Scott* notoriety, is *The Bank of Augusta v. Earle*, 13 Peters 519 (U.S., 1839), at p. 589. For the continued survival of this approval on comity, see Justice Gray in *Hilton v. Guyot*, 159 U.S. 113 (1894), at p. 163; 16 S. Ct. 139 (1895), at pp. 143f.

10   1 Ware DC 410 (Federal Case No. 11257) (Me.).

11   P. 951.

12   P. 951.

13   Pp. 953f.

14   P. 953.

15   *Conflict*, p. 116.

16   *Dred Scott*: 19 Howard 393 (U.S.). An important precursor was *Strader v. Graham*, 10 Howard 82 (U.S.), heard in 1851. The case appeared twice before the Kentucky Court of Chancery: *Graham v. Strader*, 5 Ben Monroe 173 (1846); *Strader v. Graham*, 7 Ben Monroe 633 (1847): cf. D. E. Fehrenbacher, *The Dred Scott Case* (New York, 1978), pp. 260ff. *Roe v. Wade*: 410 U.S. 113 (1973). See, e.g., L. M. Friedman, *History of American Law*, 2d ed. (New York, 1985), p. 671.

17   P. 452.

18   See chap. 3. The Northwest Ordinance of 1787 was also relevant.

19   See the cases cited in chap. 3, n. 29.

20   One might also add that for Huber slavery was not contrary to natural law: *Praelectiones juris civilis* on the *Institutes* 1.3: see A. Watson, *Slave Law in the Americas* (Athens, Ga. 1989), p. 94.

21   It will be seen that there is no need to bring into play the notion that where it was doubtful which law was applicable, the local law was to prevail.

22   For these see, above all, P. Finkelman, *An Imperfect Union: Slavery, Federalism, and Comity* (Chapel Hill, 1981).

23   For *Dred Scott*, see Justice Nelson's opinion from pp. 460ff.

24   See, above all, Chief Justice Taney, in *Scott v. Sandford*, pp. 404ff.: cf., e.g., Fehrenbacher, *Dred Scott*, pp. 295ff.

25 18 Pick. 193 (Mass, 1836).

26 P. 201. For another early case where Story was treated as giving the meaning and rights of comity, see *Willard v. The People,* 4 Scam. 461 (Ill.), at p. 471. Story's sense of comity was also the meaning attributed to the term in *Nancy Jackson v. Bulloch,* 12 Conn. 39 (1837), at 40; "It was expressly conceded that slavery was a system of such a character, that it can claim nothing by the law of comity, which prevails among friendly states upon subjects of a different class: that it was local, and must be governed entirely by the laws of the state, in which it is attempted to be enforced." The issue of comity came before Story himself, sitting in the Supreme Court in *Prigg v. Pennsylvania,* 16 Peters 539 (U.S., 1842).

27 Pp. 217f. For a southern case that accepted Story's notion of comity—though it is Kent who is cited—but held that comity would seem to require the return of a slave to his owner, on the owner's demand, from a free State, see *Neal v. Farmer,* 9 Georgia 555 (1851), at p. 572.

28 Pp. 586f.

29 We would go too far afield if we speculated on the likelihood that some free-State judges would simply have ignored or rejected Story on comity with regard to slavery if Story had followed Huber, and on the impact of this. The issue is one on which I would expect no measure of agreement from American historians and legal scholars. The problem relates to the fidelity of nineteenth-century judges to preexisting, apparently authoritative, texts.

There is a present-day particularity in American law that confuses the issue. The basic approach to legal reasoning in the Western world was shaped by events in Rome in the fifth century B.C.: For the argument see Alan Watson, *The State, Law, and Religion: Pagan Rome* (Athens, Ga., 1992). The proper route to a legal decision was to be found in an internal, legal, logic. A decision was not to appear result oriented, not to be expressly based on utilitarian considerations, nor on general principles of justice, but to be grounded on accepted legal authority or reasoning from legal authority. (I am not claiming that decisions might not at times be result oriented, but that the practice of legal reasoning was hostile to admitting this. The approach of Lord Mansfield in *Somerset's* case, which I am about to discuss, is instructive. I will argue that the decision was very result oriented, but Mansfield masked the approach behind a claim of law that did not exist.) This approach to decision reaching is to be found equally in England and the countries of western continental Europe. The acceptable authorities varied from place to place, and the strength of the tradition from time to time, but always the approach was, and is, there.

In contrast, the contemporary United States is unique in the relatively large extent to which judges may openly admit their decisions are result oriented. That, too, results from the legal tradition, but one which has in large measure broken from the rest of Western law.

One strand of this American tradition comes from legal education with the

stress on the so-called "Socratic method" and case books. To an extent un-
paralleled elsewhere, students are not exposed to a systematic treatment of
law, with clear-cut concepts, institutions, and rules, but are presented with
individual cases, outside of a historical, doctrinal, legal context but against a
background of societal interests. Since this is the culture of American scholars
involved with law, and since it is hard to see the culture one lives, they take
for granted that this is the way law does develop everywhere and at all times.
They underestimate greatly the role of doctrine and of a purely legal culture
(cf. app. E).

Another strand of this American tradition lies in the absence in early times
of formal legal education in America and the impact this had on judicial and
juristic approaches from the time when law reports were issued. The absence
of university legal education in England, it should be stressed, did not cause
the prevailing Western tradition to break.

The question that is relevant to us in the present context is purely the second strand, since the first strand appeared too late—only from Christopher
Langdell's deanship of Harvard from 1870 (R. Stevens, *Law School* [Chapel Hill,
1983], pp. 52ff.). But those who will read this book are enmeshed in the first
strand. The problem of judicial fidelity to the texts in mid-nineteenth-century
America can be resolved only when much research on the matter is done by
those aware of the standard Western tradition and of present-day legal scholarly culture. My own opinion (of course) is that American nineteenth-century
judges are credited far too much with being result oriented and that the European tradition of respect for authority that continued in the United States is
downplayed: see, e.g., Alan Watson, "The Transformation of American Property
Law: A Comparative Law Approach," 24 *Georgia Law Review* (1990), pp. 163ff.,
at pp. 186ff.

Naturally, it was argued at times that because of the federal nature of the
United States the individual States owed a particularly strict obligation of
comity to each other: see, e.g., T. R. R. Cobb, *An Inquiry into the Law of Negro
Slavery in the United States of America* (Philadelphia, 1858), pp. 183ff. In this
regard a passage of the Illinois judge Lockwood's judgment in *Willard v. The
People,* 4 Scam. 461, at pp. 475f. (1843), merits quotation:

> If the courts of this state, however, should decide that the owner of slaves
> was not protected under this law of comity, while passing through this state,
> the result would be that the emigrant with slaves could not pass through our
> borders. It needs no argument to prove that this privilege of passing through
> our state, either for business or pleasure, with their slaves, is a very great con-
> venience to our sister states, and if, after having permitted them this privilege
> for the last thirty years, we were now to deny it, could they not justly charge
> us with having availed ourselves of our local position to do them a serious
> and unnecessary injury? If the owner of slaves emigrating through this state,

without objection on our part, is not protected under this law of comity, it follows that all the slaves who have passed through this state to Missouri are free, and consequently unjustly held in bondage. The facts growing out of our geographical position, the past relations subsisting between this and neighboring states, the inconveniences to which we would subject them by a change of these relations, the loss of benefits to ourselves following a change of these relations, are such as appeal strongly to the discretion of this court.

The relations we sustain to our sister states also furnish strong reasons why the law of comity should be expanded, so as to meet the exigencies arising out of that relation. What, then, are the relations we sustain to other states which ought to affect our public policy towards them? They are not foreign states. We are bound up with them by the constitution of the United States into a Union, upon the preservation of which no one can doubt that our own peace and welfare greatly depend. Other nations may cherish friendly relations with each other, and endeavor to promote alliances and frequent intercourse, from fear of foreign war, or a desire of commercial prosperity. But to us these relations and this intercourse have a value and importance which are inestimable. They are the grounds of safety for our domestic peace, and for our hopes of the continuation of the happy government under which we live. Whatever injures one state injures the others. It is consequently our duty to consult the good of all the states, and so frame and administer our laws, that we give our sister states no real cause of offence. We ought to do them all the kind offices in our power, consistently with our duty to ourselves. Thus will be produced that concord, that union of affection, and interest among the states, which may prove an enduring cement to that happy and glorious union, upon the continuation of which our hopes of domestic peace and rational freedom so eminently depend.

By the law of nations, it would be considered just cause of complaint, if we should arbitrarily refuse to the citizens of foreign nations at peace with us permission to pass through our territories, with their property. If this be so, as regards the citizens of foreign nations, how much greater propriety does there exist that we should extend this boon, if boon it be, to our fellow citizens, who are also our friends, our neighbors and our relations. That our denial to the people of our sister states to have the right of passage for themselves and their slaves would inflict on them a most serious injury cannot be doubted.

30 Lofft 1.

31 See the discussion now above all in W. M. Wiececk,"*Somerset:* Lord Mansfield and the Legitimacy of Slavery in the Anglo-American World," 42 *University of Chicago Law Review* (1974), pp. 86ff.; *The Sources of Antislavery Constitutionalism in America, 1760–1848* (Ithaca, 1977), pp. 40ff.; Finkelman, *Imperfect Union*, pp. 16f., 38ff.; J. Oldham, "New Light on Mansfield and Slavery," (*Journal of*

British Studies 27 [1988]; 45). For the preceding view see, e.g., E. Fiddes, "Lord Mansfield and the Somersett Case," 50 *Law Quarterly Review* (1934), pp. 499ff.

32   Wiececk, "*Somerset*," p. 87. When Mansfield said "Contract for sale of slave is good here;" the word "here" does not refer to England, but means "in this instance." This is apparent from his use of "here" in the succeeding sentence. If I understand him correctly, this is not the interpretation of C. H. S. Fifoot, *Lord Mansfield* (Oxford, 1936), p. 41.

33   There exist various reports of Mansfield's opinion, but the differences between them do not concern us in the present context. But see Oldham, "New Light," pp. 55ff.

34   Francis Hargrave, a counsel for Somerset, published a short book, *An argument in the case of James Somerset, a Negro, lately determined by the Court of King's Bench* (London 1772), and he does refer to Huber at p. 47. Though the book is in the form of a speech on behalf of Somerset, the author declares it was never delivered as such. We cannot tell whether Hargrave cited Huber to Mansfield. Nor does it matter: Mansfield knew Huber well enough. Hargrave slides over the issue of *lex loci* with his reference to Huber. See also the account in 20 *Howells State Trials*, at p. 60.

35   See, e.g., Wiececk, "Somerset", p. 102.

36   See, e.g., Wiececk, "Somerset," pp. 101, 105; Oldham, "New Light," pp. 46f.

37   P. 17.

38   "New Light," p. 68.

39   In *Gedächtnisschrift für Wolfgang Kunkel*, ed. D. Nörr and D. Simon (Frankfurt am Main, 1984), pp. 37ff.

40   Mansfield's narrow judgment, which did not free the slaves in England, gave the British Parliament the opportunity (which characteristically it did not take) of legislating to control the "inconvenience."

41   Lofft 1, at pp. 17ff. Oldham prefers Serjeant Hill's version ("New Light," p. 68).

42   This point, and the absence of discussion on the very relevant notion of comity, was already noted by the sagacious Cobb, *Inquiry*, p. 171.

6   Hypotheses

1   See, e.g., A. Watson, *Legal Transplants: An Approach to Comparative Law* (Charlottesville, Va., 1974); *Society and Legal Change* (Edinburgh, 1977); *Failures of the Legal Imagination* (Philadelphia, 1988); "Comparative Law and Legal Change," 37 *Cambridge Law Journal* (1978), pp. 313ff.; "Legal Change: Sources of Law and Legal Culture," *University of Pennsylvania Law Review* (1983), pp. 1121ff.

2   A. Watson, *Slave Law in the Americas* (Athens, Ga., 1989).

3   Witness the anonymous review in 11 *American Jurist and Law Magazine* (1834), pp. 305ff., at 380ff.

4   3 Dallas (U.S., 1797), 370 at pp. 370ff.
5   See, above all, H. Jaffa, *Crisis of the House Divided* (Chicago, 1959); also e.g., C. B. Swisher, *History of the Supreme Court of the United States*, vol. 5: *The Taney Period, 1836–1864* (New York: 1974), pp. 631ff.; D. E. Fehrenbacher, *The Dred Scott Case* (New York, 1978), pp. 449ff.; J. M. McPherson, *Battle Cry of Freedom: The Civil War Era* (New York, 1988), pp. 177ff.
6   The Kansas proslavery Constitution of 1858, printed in D. W. Wilder, *The Annals of Kansas* (Topeka, 1875), pp. 134ff.; see esp. pp. 140, 146.
7   McPherson, *Battle Cry*, p. 188.
8   On the election campaign see, e.g., McPherson, *Battle Cry*, pp. 223ff.
9   See the history of events in McPherson, *Battle Cry*, pp. 234ff.
10 On the issues see, e.g., W. M. Wiececk, *The Sources of Antislavery Constitutionalism in America, 1760–1848* (Ithaca, 1977); H. M. Hyman and W. M. Wiececk, *Equal Justice under Law: Constitutional Development* (New York, 1982).
11 William L. Shirer, *The Rise and Fall of the Third Reich* (New York, 1960), p. 293. An interesting "What if?" in a legal context by a historian is Paul M. Finkelman, "The Nationalization of Slavery: A Counterfactual Approach to the 1860's," (*Louisiana Studies* 14 [1975]: 213ff).
12 Written on 8 January 1991.
13 *Imperfect Union*.
14 *Battle Cry*, pp. 170ff.
15 *Law in the United States: A General and Comparative View* (Deventer, 1988), p. 48.
16 A further counterfactual hypothesis may be envisioned. Story, let us assume, followed Huber correctly and this approach to comity was generally accepted. Nonetheless, somehow the *Dred Scott* case came before the U.S. Supreme Court, and, let us assume, Taney accepted that Scott was a free man. Lincoln and Douglas had their debates (but in a different form), Lincoln was elected president, secession and the Civil War followed. The main outlines of history would be preserved, but the writing of history would be different. *Dred Scott* would not have been among the causes of the war. I pose this hypothesis because in discussion with historians I find a reluctance on their part to accept that the doctrine of comity, which was adopted by accident, could have a profound impact on outcomes in the society. Yet historians stress *Dred Scott* among the causes of the Civil War.
17 See, above all, Watson, *Slave Law in the Americas*.
18 *The Embarrassment of Riches* (Berkeley, 1988), pp. 402ff.
19 *Embarrassment*, p. 421.
20 *Digest*, 24.1.32.13.
21 Schama has taken his reference at second hand, from L. J. van Apeldoorn, *Geschiedenis van het Nederlandsche Huwelijksrecht* (Amsterdam, 1925), p. 8 (but it should read "p. 9"). Oddly, Schama seems to have misunderstood van Apel-

doorn's point. What Grotius wrote was very different: "Marriage or matrimony is a union of man and woman for a life together, involving a lawful use of each other's body" ("Huwelick ofte echt is een verzameling van man ende wijf tot een gemeen leven, mede-brengende een wettelick gebruick van malkanders lichaem"; *Inleiding tot de Hollandsche Rechtsgeleertheyd* 1.5.1).

7   Thesis

1   See, e.g., *Roman Law and Comparative Law* (Athens, Ga., 1991), pp. 97ff. It should scarcely be necessary to state that my thesis is not that economic, political, or religious conditions have no, or very little, impact on legal change. Of course they are important. Only, the impact of legal culture is fundamental, much more so than is usually realized. It accounts for a large proportion of the rules in a legal system, for their structure and orientation. It also determines the systems from which the society will borrow (frequently without consideration of appropriateness), and the parameters of legal reasoning, whether of judges or jurists. Again, certainly, judges and jurists are involved with the general culture of their society, and this is not insignificant for legal change. But what has to be stressed is the power of the legal culture of the legal elite. See also, e.g., Alan Watson, "The Evolution of Law: Continued," 5 *Law and History Review* (1987), pp. 537ff.

For a particularly strongly argued and persuasive thesis in a different context that the main factor in the structure of legal rules was not societal conditions, see Calum Carmichael, *The Decalogues and the Laws of the Covenants* (Ithaca, 1992).

2   Statutes on other topics could, at times, be pressed into service in academic and practical argument, but these were not directly on conflicts law.

3   This, as always, they did whether or not the jurisdiction in which they were working had already adopted the same practice.

4   See, e.g., R. T. Oerton, *A Lament for the Law Commission* (Chichester, 1987).

5   Plus, occasionally, to Pothier or Pufendorf or a few others: *Doe v. Vandill*, 5 B. & C. 439 (1826); *Hog v. Lashley*, 6 Brown 577 (1792); *Potinger v. Wightman*, 3 Mer. 67 (1817).

6   On the phenomenon see, e.g., A. Watson, "The Definition of *furtum* and the Trichotomy," 28 *Tijdschrift voor Rechtsgeschiedenis* (1960), pp. 197ff.; "The Development of Marital Justifications for *malitiosa desertio* in Roman-Dutch Law," 79 *Law Quarterly Review* (1963), pp. 87ff.; *Legal Transplants, an Approach to Comparative Law* (Edinburgh, 1974), pp. 50ff.

7   For the developing Scots law see W. M. Morison, *The Decisions of the Court of Session* 11 (Edinburgh, 1811), pp. 4429ff., under the headings "Foreign" and "Forum Competens." The cases, however, are not always consistent.

8   Vol. 2, pp. 315ff.; I have taken the quotation from the third edition, which is that most appropriately dated for present purposes, 1778.

9   See above all, R. Feenstra, "Scottish-Dutch Legal Relations in the Seventeenth and Eighteenth Centuries," in *Scotland and Europe, 1200–1850*, ed. T. C. Smout (Edinburgh, 1982), pp. 128ff., and the authorities he cites; Paul Nève, "*Disputationes* of Scots Students Attending Universities in the Northern Netherlands," in *Acts of the British Legal History Conference* (1989), ed. W. M. Gordon and T. D. Fergus (London, 1991), pp. 95ff.; J. W. Cairns, "William Crosse, Regius Professor of Civil Law in the University of Glasgow, 1746–1749: A Failure of Enlightened Patronage," in *Acts of the British Legal History Conference* (1991), ed. P. Birks (London, 1992).

10 These would be by no means only of Dutch authors, given the international character of law—other than English law—at the time. My own copy of Huber, *Positiones juris* (to be discussed shortly) contains a list of books that is written in the hand of the purchaser: Mantica (1554–1614), *De conjecturis ultimarum voluntatarum*; Vinnius (1588–1657), *De pactis* and *Selectae quaestiones*; Hottoman (1524–1590), *Selectae quaestiones*; Carpzovius (1595–1666), *Practicae novae imperialis Saxonicae rerum criminalium*; Arnisaeus (died 1636?), *De republica*; Palaeotus (1524–1597), *De nothis spuriisque filiis*. Presumably these were books recommended by Huber for purchase or for reading. The two books of Vinnius, those of Lipsius and Carpzovius, have asterisks against them, possibly as being specially recommended. I doubt the asterisks represent actual purchases, because I bought from the same collection Arnisaeus, *De iure conubiorum*, an uncommon work in Scotland, and I suspect this was originally purchased in error for his *De republica*, which did not appear in the collection and which is listed but not asterisked.

    Of these jurists, presumably recommended by the Frisian Huber, only Vinnius was a fellow Dutchman, from Holland. Arnisaeus and Carpzovius were both Saxons. Hottoman was French but was also a professor in Lausanne and Strasbourg. Mantica and Pallaeotus were Italian Catholics, both cardinals in fact. It is especially noteworthy that Pallaeotus's book was widely available, since, because of its subject, it deals with matters such as the validity of marriage. The list of books also contains a specific reference to Lipsius's edition of Tacitus, *Annales* 4.10, but I have been unable to discover the significance of this.

    The first item on the list is only partially legible but seems to begin: "Jo. Desher . . ." I have been unable to decipher the meaning of this. I have found no author whose name so began. Nor does it correspond to the names of anyone matriculated at the University of Franeker or admitted to the Faculty of Advocates at the relevant times: cf. *Album Studiosorum Academiae Franekerensis*, vol. 1, ed. S. J. Fockema Andreae and Th. J. Meijer (Franeker, 1968); *Faculty of Advocates Minute Book*, vol. 1, ed. J. M. Pinkerton (Edinburgh, 1976).

    The purchaser need not have been matriculated to be a student of Huber's: if he were matriculated, he could only be R. Bethune (matriculated 24 October 1684: *Album*, p. 236) or Andreas Bruce (matriculated 5 July 1683: *Album*,

p. 232). No English student matriculated in law at the relevant times.

Indeed, at that time (from 1682), Huber had a special position with all the qualifications of a professor without being one. Many students who came to Franeker to hear Huber lecture privately in his home did not enroll in the university, and this was to be the cause of a famous conflict. See G. C. J. J. van den Bergh, *The Life and Work of Gerard Noodt (1647–1725): Dutch Legal Scholarship between Humanism and Enlightenment* (Oxford, 1988), pp. 50ff.; cf. R. Feenstra, "De Franeker juridische faculteit in nationaal en internationaal perspectief," in *Universiteit te Franeker, 1585–1811*, ed. G. Th. Jensma, F. R. H. Smit, and F. Westra (Leeuwarden, 1985), pp. 289ff., at pp. 289, 296.

11   *Commentaries on American Law*, vol. 2, 12th ed. (1873), p. 455, note b.

12   The price of sixteen pounds sterling is impossibly high. One possible explanation is that the writer intended sixteen Scottish pounds, which would then be the equivalent of one pound, nine and one-half pence of English money (H. A. Grueber, *Handbook of the Coins of Great Britain and Ireland* [London, 1899], p. liii). But thirty-six Dutch florins would not translate as sixteen pounds Scots. Perhaps the figures represent the total cost of books bought at the suggestion of Huber.

Books in Holland were not particularly expensive. The third Culloden could write on 10 January 1693 to his son John (later known as Bumper John), in Rotterdam: "As to your resolution of learning latin and french and buying books of great expense in order thereto, you may also spare that to me, [i.e., I need no accounting from you] for you may drink as much at a doun-sitting, without being very much debaucht as would compass all the necessary expense, such books requyres" (*More Culloden Papers*, ed. D. Warrand, 1 [Inverness, 1923], p. 225).

13   The National Library of Scotland has part 3 of Huber's *Praelectiones*, published at Franeker, 1690; and the whole work, Leipzig, 1707, and Louvain, 1766. Of this work, Edinburgh University Library has editions of 1735 (Leipzig) and 1749 (Frankfurt). Of the *Positiones*, the National Library has the Leipzig edition of 1685, Edinburgh University Library has the Franeker edition of 1710.

14   J. Voet: *Simon Lord Lovat v. James Lord Forbes*, M. 4512 (1742); *Kerr v. Alexander Earl of Home*, M. 4522 (1771); *Edwards v. Prescot*, M. 4535 (1720); *Sinclair and Sutherland v. Frazer*, M. 4542 (1768); *Morison and Others v. Earl of Sutherland*, M. 4595 (1749) (and the same case M. 4598), *Brunsdone v. Wallace* M. 4784 (1789); *Dodds v. Westcomb*, M. 4793 (1745). Rodenburgh: *Christie v. Straiton*, M. 4569 (1746) (and the same case, M. 4571); *Morison and Others v. Earl of Sutherland*, M. 4595 (1749) (and the same case M. 4598).

15   M. 4533.

16   M. 4451. But *Kinloch v. Fullerton*, M. 4456 (1739), indicates that this approach to *comitas* was not universal. *Comitas* in *Norris v. Wood*, M. 4466 (1743), and *Laycock v. Clark*, M. 4554 (1767), is to the same effect whether on the view of Huber or of the other Dutch jurists.

17 Respectively, M. 4512, M. 4520, M. 4542, M. 4522.

18 *Oratio Inauguralis in Aperienda Jurisconsultorum Bibliotheca* (1689); see the edition of Edinburgh, 1989, p. 67, with nn. 29 and 32 by J. W. Cairns.

19 For the impact of Lord Mansfield on the development of English conflict of laws, see, e.g. (in addition to chap. 4), Cheshire and North's *Private International Law*, 11th ed., P. M. North and J. J. Fawcett (London, 1987), pp. 24ff.; A. E. Anton, "The Introduction into English Practice of Continental Theories on the Conflict of Laws," 5 *International and Comparative Law Quarterly* (1956), pp. 534ff., at pp. 538ff.; C. P. Rodgers, "Continental Literature and the Development of the Common Law by the King's Bench: c. 1750–1800," in *Courts and the Development of Common Law*, ed. V. Piergiovanni (Berlin, 1987), pp. 161ff., at pp. 182ff.

20 The best biography is still John Lord Campbell, *The Lives of the Chief Justices of England.* I have used the 3d edition (London, 1874), 3:157ff.

21 See, e.g., Campbell, *Lives*, 3:197ff., 312ff.

22 See, e.g., Campbell, *Lives*, 3:411ff.

23 For civilian works cited by Mansfield see Rodgers, "Continental Literature," pp. 166ff. "A Catalogue of Lord Mansfield's Books in Lincoln's Inn Fields, June 1793" exists, but its provenance has not been fully determined (Rodgers, "Continental Literature," pp. 169f.). Rodgers lists the continental books (including two volumes of Huber's *Praelectiones*) in the inventory ("Continental Literature," pp. 171f.).

Appendix A   Huber's Positiones Juris

1 "De Franeker juridische fakulteit in nationaal en internationaal perspectief," in *Universiteit te Franeker 1585–1811*, ed. G. Th. Jensma, F. R. H. Smit, and F. Westra (Leeuwarden, 1985), pp. 289ff., at p. 296.

2 "22. Hodie per Europam, frequens et difficilis est quaestio: si negotium alibi inchoatum, alibi exitum habeat, utrius loci jura saepe diversa et pugnantia servanda sint. de Rebuspub. diversis loquimur, in eadem Republ. ut apud Romanos, uno olim Imperio, haec res usum non habet.

"23. Prima et summa regula est: nulla lex valet extra suum territorium, et omnis lex obligat eos, qui in territorio legislatoris reperiuntur *arg. 1. ult. d. Iurisd.* etiam peregrinos per *1. 7. §.10. in fin. d. Interdict: et releg.*

"24. Hinc forma celebrandi actus inter vivos aut mortis causa, juxta ritum loci, in quo actus celebratur, etiam ab exteris, institui debet, ac ita perfectus aut non, valet aut non valet, ubique locorum. *Gail.* 1. 2. obs. 123. *Sande* 1.4. tit.1. def. 14."

3 On the other hand we see how great an injustice Livermore did Huber. Here Huber cites not only Rodenburgh and Sande, but also Gail, Argentraeus, and Burgundus.

Appendix B   James Kent's First Edition

1   See, e.g., J. A. C. Thomas, *Textbook of Roman Law* (Amsterdam, 1970), p. 259.
2   Vol. 10, §79 (p. 103 in the fourth, Belgian, edition of 1824).
3   *Traité des obligations*, article préliminaire.

Appendix C   The Case of The Ship Columbus

1   Pp. 82ff.
2   P. 114.
3   Pp. 115f.
4   For the practice see, e.g., G. C. J. J. van den Bergh, *The Life and Work of Gerard Noodt (1647–1725)* (Oxford, 1988), pp. 137ff.
5   Disapprobation of Huber is not the sole recorded example of Sir James Marriott's "pedantic folly" (*Dictionary of National Biography*, vol. 12 [Oxford, 1917], pp. 1083f.).

Appendix D   Story, Beale, and Moveable Property

1   *A Treatise on the Conflict of Laws*, vol. 2 (New York, 1935), p. 978.
2   Story, *Conflict*, pp. 308ff.; J. Voet, *Commentarius ad Pandectas* 38.17.34; 1.4.2.11; P. Voet, *De statutis eorumque concursu*, 4.2.n.6; 9.1.8; Hertius, *De collisione legum* 4n.6; Bynkershoek, *Quaestiones juris privati* 1.10; Huber, *Praelectiones juris romani et hodierni* 2.1.3.13.
3   P. 27.
4   P. 690.
5   Pp. 451f.
6   *Hunter v. Potts*, 4 T.R. 182, at p. 192; *Marsh v. Hutchinson*, 2 Bos & Pul. 229n. (admittedly a case from the Scottish Court of Session but Thurlow's strong statement seems to be of general import); *Phillips v. Hunter*, 2 H. Black. 402, at p. 405.
7   *Harvey v. Richards*, 1 Mason 381 (Federal Case No. 6184) (Circuit Court, D. Mass.).
8   P. 224. See also, e.g., *Goodwin v. Jones*, 3 Mass. 514 (1807), at p. 517; *Milne v. Moreton*, 6 Binn. 353 (Pa. 1814), at p. 301; *Andrews v. Herriot*, 4 Cowen 508 (N.Y. 1825), at note, p. 517; *Blake v. Williams*, 6 Pick. 286 (Mass. 1828), at p. 314.
9   Beale also stressed that for intangibles the maxim *mobilia sequuntur personam* was losing much of its force (*Treatise* 2, p. 979). But this was already well known to Story, *Conflict*, p. 315. See above all, *Milne v. Moreton*, 6 Binn. 353 (Pa. 1814), per Chief Justice Edward Tilghman, at p. 361.
10   See the references that Beale gives, *Treatise* 2, pp. 981ff.
11   Pp. 269ff.

12   The citation should be to *Barton v. Waters*, 1 Cold. 450 (Tenn.).
13   *Conflict*, pp. 487ff.
14   Pp. 1ff.

Appendix E   Doctrinal Legal History

1   By the same token, of course, my views on legal change and the relationship of law and society cannot be accepted by most American legal historians, because to a considerable extent my views depend on sources that cannot be read. Moreover, since in this book I am arguing that Story misunderstood Huber, why should I be given the benefit of the doubt? Is it not more likely that it is I who misunderstood Huber?
2   Second ed. (New York, 1985), p. 330.
3   *History*, p. 332.
4   See A. Watson, *Roman Law and Comparative Law* (Athens, Ga., 1991), pp. 166ff.
5   See A. Watson, "The Transformation of American Property Law: A Comparative Law Approach," 24 *Georgia Law Review* (1990), pp. 163ff.

Index of Sources

General Index

This book may be kept

FOURTEEN DAYS

A fine will be charged for each day the book is kept overtime.

GAYLORD 142

PRINTED IN U S A